QUICK, EASY
STRATEGIES FOR
SUCCESS IN
ANY SPEAKING
SITUATION

WINNING
WHEN IT REALLY COUNTS

ARCH LUSTBERG
PHOTOGRAPHS BY ANDREA MOHIN

Simon and Schuster
New York   London   Toronto   Sydney   Tokyo

Copyright © 1988 by Arch Lustberg
All rights reserved
including the right of reproduction
in whole or in part in any form.
Published by Simon and Schuster
A Division of Simon & Schuster Inc.
Simon & Schuster Building
Rockefeller Center
1230 Avenue of the Americas
New York, NY 10020

SIMON AND SCHUSTER and colophon are
registered trademarks
of Simon & Schuster Inc.

DESIGNED BY BARBARA MARKS
Manufactured in the United States of America

10 9 8 7 6 5 4 3 2 1

Library of Congress Cataloging in Publication Data
Lustberg, Arch.

Winning when it really counts: quick, easy strategies for success
in any speaking situation / Arch Lustberg; photographs by Andrea Mohin.
p.   cm.
Includes index.
1. Public speaking.   I. Title.
PN4121.L78 1988
808.5′1—dc19   88-11551
                        CIP
ISBN 0-671-55241-4

CONTENTS

INTRODUCTION

Almost any situation can seem tough if you're unprepared for it or unsure of yourself. The toughest of all are those high-pressure situations that can make or break a career—the one-on-one job interview, the sales presentation to the million-dollar account, the sudden and unexpected contract negotiation, the defense of a budget before a hostile committee, the request to be a substitute speaker at an important banquet. The list is as endless as our capacity to worry.

Yet, the one thing I've learned after years of working with people in business, education, and the professions is that with enough confidence, a few simple skills, and just a touch of personal style, you can come across as a winner whenever it's your turn to speak. There are a few quick, easy strategies you can learn to help you through almost any speaking situation. And remember that even the best memo or report carries less weight than the ability to convince and persuade in person.

Every speaking situation involves a person who is selling his ideas and himself to another person or group of people. Once you make that fundamental connection, you are well on your way to becoming a persuasive speaker. Think of speech as an information transplant. A mouth in motion is useless unless the mind of the listener is getting the exact message exactly as it's intended. I made this point in two booklets, each dealing with a practical situation where it is crucial to get a message across. "Testifying with Impact" (1982) and "Winning at Confrontation" (1984) were both published by the U.S. Chamber of Commerce. I've had a lot of mail from people who read one or both of those booklets telling me how much they've been helped, and it encouraged me to widen the scope of the present book to include almost every make-or-break speaking situation so you will learn to handle yourself with style, class, and ease.

It is not enough to be honest, hardworking, and dedicated— you can still lose. To be a winning speaker, your audience must come away saying, "I believe that person," "I trust that person," "I like that person." So this book is broken down into two parts: the skills and techniques needed to be a winning speaker, and how to apply those techniques in special situations, when winning really counts.

I want you to be able to face a lot of different scenarios— some predictable, some unanticipated—and come out on top. I want you to understand and recognize that winning communication depends not only on improving your basic skills but also using them effectively to accomplish your career goals. Speech is getting results. In short, I want to help you change your thinking about the way you approach speaking *and* the way you speak.

You can have the best message in the world, but if you don't present that message well, you lose.

People enjoy listening to a skillful, enthusiastic speaker. They enjoy being part of a friendly presentation. When your audience glows, you win; and when people get your message, when they go away fully informed, you also win. And so do they.

I'm not going to waste your time with a lot of tedious vowel exercises, discussions of dipthongs, and all the other technical baggage of conventional speech books. Instead, I'll show you:

- How to use your face, your body, and your voice to project warmth and confidence in tough speaking situations
- How to prepare and rehearse what you want to say
- How to think on your feet
- How to sell your point of view
- How to explain your position rather than deny accusations
- How to handle confrontation and hostility and make yourself the person everyone is rooting for
- How to handle yourself during job interviews and company meetings
- How to master winning negotiation and sales techniques
- How to get others as enthusiastic about your ideas as you are
- And much, much more.

And I guarantee you'll come out a winner—when it really counts!

BECOMING A WINNER

1

WINNING

WITH STYLE

Style is what makes you unique.

The best speakers have style; they're one of a kind. The worst speakers lack style; they're a dime a dozen.

Every speaker with no style looks like every other one. Think about it. You can't tell one dull politician or state department spokesperson or presidential press secretary or TV interviewee from another. Every dull teacher and preacher seems to be a clone of every other one. Unfortunately, it's easier to be dull.

WE ARE WHAT WE EXPERIENCE

Speech is an acquired habit. We weren't born with language skills or speech skills; we learned them. So we take on the speech characteristics of the people we're in constant contact with—parents, teachers, friends, role models. We imitate untrained, often poor speakers instead of developing our own style.

But you don't have to be a dull speaker. You can learn techniques, develop skills and confidence, learn how to prepare yourself, and become a really effective and interesting communicator. But above all, you have to devote time and attention to being yourself while speaking.

Most of us don't know how to be ourselves in formal speaking situations. We develop what I call a platform personality. It comes from watching one unskilled speaker after another. We pick up their bad habits.

Here's what we see and what we do. We approach the microphone. Because it isn't a natural situation to be in, we clear our throats. Our throats don't *need* clearing but we do it. It's become a habit, and a bad one at that. And every subsequent act is another bad habit. We tighten our facial muscles. We place our voices further back in the throat than necessary. We stiffen our head and neck muscles. We make a louder sound than we have to, probably in order to guarantee that any sound will come out. We have just taken on a "professional characterization." We want to look and sound serious, important, intelligent, impressive, and instead we come across as pompous.

A nurse wrote to me, "You're right. Whenever I got up to

speak in public I thought I had to impress people. So I became professional, serious, insufferable. It's great to know that I should be *me*. You made me realize that I should stop trying to impress my audience. If I *express* my thoughts really well, they'll remember what I say. You helped me find my personal style."

A year or so after the 1984 election, Geraldine Ferraro said that she may have made a mistake by trying too hard to project strength. Exactly right, Ms. Ferraro. Most of the people I know who had personal contact with Walter Mondale in that same election describe him as warm, friendly, and personable. I've been told the same thing about George Bush, but you and I never saw those qualities in all their public appearances. They tried too hard to look presidential and turned us off.

My point is that, unfortunate as it may be, we have to recognize that today style has become at least as important a communication tool as substance. I'm not applauding nor condoning that fact, but it *is* a fact. Now that we're getting our communication mostly through close-up pictures with sound, the person who looks pleasant and sounds nice often gets elected, promoted, convinces the jury, and just plain *wins*.

Because so many of today's business leaders never had the benefit of really good speech training, I've heard executive after executive complain, "The company spent tens of thousands of dollars on bringing us together for a meeting and all the leaders who spoke put us to sleep." They were just plain dull. They brought no personality, no individuality, no *style* to their presentations. They droned on . . . and on . . . and on.

One board chairman I worked with was guilty of exactly that—being dull in his speeches to "the troops." At annual meeting after annual meeting, he was supposed to communicate his excitement about the company's prospects for the coming year. And he *was* excited about the future. But his speaking skills weren't developed. When he said, "I'm proud of what we've done," he sounded as if his mayonnaise was spoiled and looked as if he was going to throw up, and he destroyed his message. His colleagues were bored to death and believed his apparent lack of conviction in what he was saying. But he felt he had to look calm, restrained, serious, and professional in front of his people. *He must not make an ass of himself in public.* Ironically, they all knew that when he was talking about his favorite baseball team he was alive, dynamic, excited, animated. He found it terribly hard to believe that he could talk about his professional team with as much excitement and enthusiasm as he could about his sports team. But then, after watching his performance on videotape, he finally realized that putting his baseball spirit into his corporate speech was not acting. He wasn't looking foolish in front of his colleagues; he was actually doing what he really wanted to do—communicate his real, genuine excitement about the company's future prospects.

It isn't easy when you've been doing it wrong all your life. We all know that bad habits are hard to break. But once you learn good speaking techniques the *real you* can come through.

▪YOUR OPTIONS

You can't be loved by everyone. You can't come across to everyone as a brilliant communicator. But you can develop your style so that you'll be liked by a lot of people. After all, the people in your audience have only four choices:

They can like you
They can dislike you
They can not care about you one way or the other
Or they can feel sorry for you

You have a better chance of being liked if you're yourself—natural, comfortable. If you're liked, you'll get your message across. And if you get your message across, you'll be believed. It's a wonderful road map to winning.

Law firms are discovering that speech training can be very effective in preparing witnesses. It can make all the difference in the final outcome of a trial. The courtroom is an unnatural setting for people like you and me. We're used to seeing films and TV shows in which witnesses are badgered, harassed, and reduced to blithering idiots by skilled attorneys. So we start with a totally negative approach to communication. As soon as we understand that we can be ourselves—and be far more convincing to a jury and a judge as ourselves—we're able to give better testimony. Certainly, the same is true of being interviewed on radio and television. It's true of standing delivering a speech at a lectern. It's true of conducting a meeting or speaking up as a participant in that meeting.

Style makes the difference even among members of the clergy. How did Reverend Robert Schuller get a congregation of millions, while a local minister may be preaching to a half-empty church? Jimmy Swaggart is another very popular TV evangelist, as are Billy Graham, Pat Robertson, and Jerry Falwell. Do you like one of them better than the others? Do you dislike any of them? The difference is style. Each one appeals to a tremendous following. Yet each runs the risk and *accepts the reality* that not everyone will love him. So each is not afraid to be the person he wants to be in front of an audience. And each is liked by a huge constituency.

TV commercials are the last word in style, or at least they reflect the styles that the advertising agencies think will sell products. Some do and some don't. But the memorable commercials are invariably the ones with stylistic impact. The two men who play the owners of Bartles & Jaymes Wine Coolers were hired because they look and sound like nonactors, real people. They got the assignment because the agency wanted a specific style and they were able to deliver it. On the other hand, his agency convinced Lee Iacocca that he was the best one to deliver his message with authority since he *was* authority. You probably wouldn't believe how many actors are auditioned for most commercials until one is found with the exact style the agency is looking for.

If you've ever watched Willard Scott do the weather on NBC you know exactly what I mean. He's folksy, down-home, even corn-pone, but a lot of people are tuned in just to watch Willard wish 103-year-old Emma Mae Jones a happy birthday. He's the first to admit he's outlandish, but it's his *style*.

You've seen the car dealer who points his finger menacingly at you, talks too loud and too fast, and sort of dares you to come to his dealership and buy your new car. It's his *style*. You've seen the movie critic with a mop of hair and a mustache that would circle the earth twice around the equator. It's part of his *style*.

You may like them. You may dislike them. But with their style you remember them.

BE YOURSELF

Someone else's style won't work for you. You really don't want to be someone else, and your audience certainly doesn't want you to try to be anyone else.

So, above all, style is being yourself. But you're very likely to think that's not enough. You may be naturally shy, introverted, not very articulate, and not really able to think on your feet. You certainly want to change that impression in front of an audience. And you can. You can learn the skills and techniques that will enable you to create the impression you want to create. You can learn to say what you want to say in the way you really want to say it—in a way that will still be true to yourself while getting the substance of your message across to your audience. That's *your* style. It's your trademark. You can use it. And it will prove to be your strongest tool in achieving your career goals and in improving all your relationships.

WINNING

WITH SKILL: USING YOUR FACE

The most important element of style is your face.

This wasn't always the case. Before film and television brought us the close-up, the public speaker was almost always separated from his audience by a lot of distance. The audience was lucky to get close enough to make out the speaker's features. So, from the beginning of time to the advent of the camera, the voice was the dominant force in speech. The great speaker was the one with the dynamite voice, the "golden tones," the orator who captivated the audience with vocal power and style.

Not any more. Now we can see every detail of the speaker's face in living color and those "golden tones" are likely to come across as phony.

We make an immediate judgment when we look at someone's face for the first time. As soon as it sees you, your audience will form an opinion of you.

How often have you said or heard one of these comments? "I don't like his looks." "I don't trust him." "He looks sneaky to me." "If I didn't know him, I wouldn't believe him."

We make dozens of statements like this every day, statements that prejudge another person based on appearance alone. And inevitably a person or an audience seeing you for the first time is going to make a judgment of you based exclusively on your face, even before you have uttered a single word. That's why the face is the single most important factor in spoken communication (with the possible exception of radio broadcasting and telephone conversations, when you can't see the person who is talking). The face and the voice always work together in their effect on an audience. Let me amend this by saying that the face and the voice *should* always work together. If your face is saying one thing and your voice is saying something else, there's an automatic short circuit between you and your listeners. Which message are they supposed to believe? If your face and your voice convey the *same* message, there will be no question in anyone's mind that you mean what you say and that you're saying what you mean.

▪THE SMILE

The face has a wide range of expressions that can either confirm or contradict what we're saying, but by far the most prominent is the smile.

We smile when we're happy, when we're having a good time.
We smile a lot when we like the person we're talking to and
the subject is pleasant.
We smile when we know we're right.
We smile when we have the upper hand.

But watch out. A smile has to be genuine. It has to be appropriate. If it isn't both, it can't be effective and it won't be believed. In fact, it will work against you.

Former President Jimmy Carter comes to mind immediately. We got used to seeing him grin at the most inappropriate times. It almost seemed as though he was smiling as he said the words *nuclear war*. Nothing to smile about there.

Senator Lugar of Indiana has a similar expression. He also seems to be grinning when he's not. He was our observer to the Marcus–Aquino election in the Philippines. He returned home and with what looked like a big grin said, "This election was dominated by fraud." He seemed to be rejoicing in that fact.

Of course, there is such a thing as the polite smile we often use to conceal our real thoughts and feelings and the "stiff-upper-lip" smile. But, if the smile doesn't come easily or naturally, if it isn't appropriate to what you are saying, and what you want your listener to believe, don't force it.

THE OPEN FACE

Even more important than the smile is what I call an open face. People who speak with an open face appear to be honest. They appear believable. They seem to be trustworthy, confident, self-assured. But under the stress of speaking situations, we tend to forget that the face is sending messages that may be even more powerful than our words.

Basically, there are three possible facial positions or expres-

YOU LOSE when you speak with what I call the **closed face.** Your audience will think you're mad at them.

sions. I call them the closed face, the neutral face, and the open face.

The closed face results from the creation of a vertical line between the brows, the frown line. We do this involuntarily when we draw our eyes into partially closed narrow slits and tighten the muscles of the brow. Many of us do this when we think. It's the expression we get when we're worried. Most of us look that way when we're angry. It's a terrible expression for an audience to see.

The neutral face has a "dead" look. Absolutely nothing moves but the mouth when we speak with the neutral face. If you look in the mirror and count aloud to five with absolutely no expression and no animation, you'll be watching yourself speak with a neutral

YOU LOSE when you speak with a **neutral face.** You may be trying to look serious, but to your audience you'll look dead.

face. Without realizing it, this is the facial position most of us assume when we speak in a public setting.

Next time you're watching television, notice how little movement you see in the faces of the White House correspondents for each of the networks. Sam Donaldson, Bill Plante, and Chris Wallace hardly even move their lips as they speak. You almost *never see their upper teeth.* They look as if they've just been released from coffins for this broadcast and will be lowered back into the ground when it's over.

One of our most brilliant journalists is George Will. He has a great mind, but I doubt that he'll ever achieve a high degree of popularity as a TV commentator, since his face is either closed, because he's trying to look very serious, or neutral, because he

YOU WIN when you speak with an **open face**—eyebrows raised and eyes open, looking directly at your audience. And don't forget to smile, if it's appropriate.

wants to appear impartial. Will, like most other trained journalists, rarely smiles on television and almost never opens his face. A recent Los Angeles *Times-Mirror* survey indicated that very few people recognize him, even though he's been on ABC for several years. In fact, the survey referred to him as the invisible commentator. You have to admire his superior mind and his wonderful writing ability but not his oral communication skills.

The open face is the name I give to the creation of the horizontal lines in the forehead by elevating the eyebrows and holding that position for a short time. We open our face a lot when we're in animated conversation. We open our face constantly when we're talking to a baby or playing with a kitten or a puppy. We open our face when we're telling a favorite story. But in more formal speaking situations, stress and bad habits, like trying to look serious and professional, prevent us from opening our face.

It's a technique anyone can learn, however, because it involves doing something consciously that all of us do quite naturally when we're not thinking about communicating. And you'll be amazed at the difference in your appearance when you look at yourself speak in the three facial positions. What you'll see in the mirror when you practice this technique is what your audience will see when it watches you speak.

Try it. As an exercise, look at yourself in the mirror. Draw your brow into a deep frown. Tighten your facial muscles. Narrow your eyes. Purse your lips. Now say aloud the words "Good morning." Notice how unattractive you look. Notice, too, how unpleasant and hostile you sound.

Now try the neutral face. Relax all your facial muscles. Let absolutely nothing register on your face. You might as well be sleeping for all the animation your face is now showing. Make sure now that you barely move your lips as you say to your mirror "Good morning." Dull.

Now, try to open your face. Elevate your eyebrows. Let the horizontal lines appear in your brow. If you're having trouble creating an open face, think about talking to a baby. Now, quietly say the same two words to the image in the mirror, "Good morning." It's a wonderful change. It's warm. It's friendly. It's an invitation, a welcome. If you look that way in a speaking situation, it makes a remarkable difference in the impression you create on your audience. When you feel comfortable opening your face in front of an audience, you'll be believed. You'll be trusted. You'll appear to be in control of yourself and the situation. You'll be a winner. Just by using the open face, you can bring instant life to your delivery. Why settle for anything less?

In the last chapter I spoke about the board chairman who learned to bring animation and enthusiasm into his speeches to the troops. I videotaped him as he delivered a typical speech in his typical manner, and when I played it back, even he was bored. Then we talked about the open face and I videotaped him again as he delivered the same speech. He didn't change a word. All he did was use an open face, and he was terrific.

But, like the smile, the open face has to be genuine and appropriate. You have no desire to look bug-eyed to your audience, nor should your eyebrows move up and down in a jerky rhythm. That will remind the audience of Groucho flicking the ash off his long cigar and making a fast exit. But if you're saying a word like "wonderful" or a sentence like "I had a wonderful time," your audience will get the message better and believe you if your face is open as you say it.

The open face also tends to disguise all our warts, because an audience becomes attentive to the ideas of the speaker whose face is open. Think back on the presidential election of 1984. Walter Mondale's face was almost never open and, obviously, the American public tuned him out. People noticed the bags under Mondale's eyes. They noticed the downward turn of his mouth. Why? Because nothing was happening on his face that was pleasant and interesting to look at as he spoke to them. So they noticed his blemishes.

⸀THE MUSTACHE AND THE BEARD

This brings me to facial hair. For those of you who wear a black or very dark mustache or beard, the open face is vital. In the old movies, the villain always wore a mustache and the hero was always clean shaven. Even today, law enforcement officers have a "profile" of likely criminals, and judging from the cars stopped on the highway and the travelers whose bags get checked thoroughly at customs, people with black facial hair (and long hair) fit the "suspect profile." As unfair as it might be, realize that such a prejudice exists. I'm not suggesting you shave off your facial hair. But I am suggesting that one of the surest ways to come across pleasantly and make audiences forget their facial-hair bias is to use an open face with consistency as you speak. Incidentally, a gray or white beard, if neat, usually creates a favorable impression. I've never been to dinner with a gray-bearded man when *he* wasn't given the check by the waiter.

If you've never noticed open faces before, watch Alan Alda, Burt Reynolds, Bill Cosby. Their faces are almost always open. They're likable. They're warm and friendly. They're believable. They're among the most successful actors of our time. They're winners. Use an open face and you can be, too.

WINNING

WITH SKILL: USING GESTURES

Just as I crusade for the open face, so I strongly advocate the use of an open body. But, in stressful speaking situations, it's probably even more difficult for us to open up our bodies and use our hands than it is to open our faces.

YOU LOSE when you speak in the **fig-leaf** position. (What are you trying to hide?)

Or when you thrust your hands in your pockets and rattle your change.

Gesture is the key to the open body, and it's a terribly difficult concept for many people to cope with. Stress not only induces us to neutralize our faces but also to *hide* our hands. Our hands and faces are naked, and we tend to put them away when stress hits. In natural situations like relaxed conversation, we gesture to emphasize almost everything we say. In fact, the gesture helps us make the emphasis; but in formal speaking, we almost never relax enough to use our hands.

▪ THE NO-NOS

We clutch the lectern, if there is one. Or, if there isn't a lectern, one hand clutches the other wrist in front of the crotch. This

Or when you fold your arms across your chest—the female fig leaf.

Or when you clasp your hands behind your back like Prince Charles. Don't hide your hands. **Use** them.

position is called the fig leaf and most men tend to home in on it when they're standing in front of an audience. Those who don't use the fig leaf thrust their hands in their pockets—men in their trousers, women in their jackets—or fold their arms in front of them or they hide their hands behind their backs.

But we all talk with our hands. If they aren't free as they are in conversation, fingers gesture for us or elbows jerk into strange contortions. In the fig-leaf position, if we open our hands to emphasize a point and come right back to the fig leaf, we look like "flashers." If we flick fingers from the fig leaf, the movement looks ridiculous if not obscene.

And how about the hands deep in the pockets? We've all seen the speaker who digs his hands as far down in his pockets as

YOU LOSE when you speak with uptight gestures like these—from fig leaf . . .

. . . to flasher.

they'll go and then proceeds to talk with his hands moving excitedly *inside the pockets*. Gestures in this position look ridiculous. The person who plays with his keys and his change looks even more ridiculous. And who can pay attention to what he is saying with a distraction like that? Yet, many people do it.

Why? First of all, most of us don't know what to do with our hands. Second, we've been told from childhood, "Don't talk with your hands." Wrong! A woman in one of my training sessions came up to me during a break and said, "But, Arch, I never talk with my hands." As she said the word *talk*, her hands came up slightly from her sides. And on the word *hands*, her hands came out, palms up, and reached half the distance between us. She gestured twice in that one sentence, believing all the while that she really never talked with her hands.

Like opening our faces, when we *think* about gesture, we tend not to be able to do it at all or we tend to do it wrong. And, like the smile and the open face, the gesture must be genuine and appropriate. A genuine gesture means that it looks natural. Appropriate means that it fits what you say and happens at exactly the right time. One of the great comic mistakes of our time is letting the local merchant or businessman do his own TV commercials. He's usually stiff, unnatural, and uncomfortable to be out of his natural habitat. TV cameras, microphones, lights, makeup, and acting are all out of his area of expertise. So, the poor guy stands there, reading a script and gesturing awkwardly and incorrectly on the wrong words. Every hand movement and vocal inflection are wrong. And you either dislike, feel sorry for, or laugh at him. Genuine and appropriate gestures are the ones we use when we move our hands, bodies, and heads the way we do in ordinary everyday conversation.

THE CLASSIC GESTURES

The classic gestures are the handshake and the embrace. Each says, "I want to get closer to you . . . I want to share me with you . . . I want you to share you with me." A genuine gesture is the speaker's equivalent of a *hug. I hug you with this idea.* It's a speaker's way of closing the physical gap with the audience without invading anyone else's space.

Like the woman who said she never talks with her hands, a lot of us were told by parents, friends, or colleagues, "Don't be so dramatic. You're too theatrical. Stop using your hands so much." So we become even more self-conscious and reluctant to use a really necessary communication weapon. One woman said that the nuns who taught her in grade school actually had her sit on her hands so she wouldn't be quite so demonstrative.

YOU LOSE when you overwhelm your audience with exaggerated gestures from what I call "The John Madden School of Sports Broadcasting for the Hard of Hearing and Visually Impaired."

Remember, communication is the transfer of ideas from your mind to other minds. When these minds are distracted or when they're falling asleep, the communication is obviously failing. It lacks some necessary ingredient. Remember also that communication should be an intellectual act of love. "I want my message to penetrate your mind. I want you to want to receive my message. And I want to do nothing that will distract you from understanding my message effortlessly."

So try this exercise. Stand in front of a full-length mirror. Be sure your face is expressionless and your hands stay absolutely still. Now in the dullest possible voice, say the words "I had a wonderful time." It sounds as though you might be saying, "I

25

think I'm catching the flu." Now open your face and move your hands, palms upward, on the word *wonderful*, and say the same sentence. Everything comes to life. You're adding good old-fashioned energy to your communication. Now it begins to sound and look as if you mean what you're saying and that you're saying what you mean.

When stress dominates your communication, there's rarely any evidence of gesture. You need to force yourself to use gestures in order to seem natural in this most unnatural of situations, just as you need to force yourself to open your face, because they won't happen by themselves.

Television commercials can be fun to watch from this new perspective. You'll wonder, as I do, how directors can allow such strange use of hands. My favorite current incorrect use of gesture (neither genuine nor appropriate) happens in a Preparation H commercial. The box appears on the screen. The Magic Marker is seen circling the words "pain and itching." The idea is established firmly in the audience's mind that hemorrhoids *hurt* and they *itch*. Then we see two hands spread far apart and we hear a voice say "Preparation H shrinks swollen membranes." On the word *shrinks*, we see the hands move from about twelve inches apart to about eight inches apart, leaving the vivid impression that the shrunken membranes are still *enormous*. A more appropriate gesture would show two fingers (thumb and forefinger), separated by about an inch, coming together on the word *shrink*.

I've also wondered about the Cliff Robertson ads for AT&T. He is a wonderful choice—a warm, friendly, sincere man. But his early spots for AT&T showed him with folded arms during long periods of talking. He appeared to be the antithesis of open. And this was for the company that prided itself on its "Reach out and touch someone" campaign. Neither the actor nor the director realized that folded arms were not what the company really wanted to communicate to its customers.

Your gestures are perceived by your audience as a burst of

YOU WIN when you speak with an open face and appropriate gestures. The gesture is your way of embracing your audience.

energy. Again, it's the communicator's equivalent of a hug, a movement in the direction of the audience. You seem natural. You seem to be loving them. And you know what? They love you back. They're saying, "Thank you for taking the trouble to really get your message across to me. Thank you for keeping me interested, awake, and alert." Next time you're listening to a talk, notice how animated and enthusiastic the audience is when the speaker has an open face and uses appropriate gestures. And notice how totally numb the audience is when the speaker lacks these two essential techniques for dynamic delivery.

CHAPTER

4

WINNING

WITH SKILL:
USING YOUR
VOICE

I've always considered it remarkable that voice is taught as a separate course in high school and college. I can understand separating voice as part of a drama or music curriculum, but in speech courses, voice has no business being separated from the mind, the face, and the body. In other words, voice should never be taught in a vacuum.

Let's go back to the facial exercise you tried earlier. Close your face and say, "Good morning." Now open your face, elevate your eyebrows, and quietly say the same two words. Your voice takes on the condition of your face. If your face is closed, your voice closes and tightens. If your face opens, your voice opens, warms, and caresses. Your voice almost always follows the lead of your face and body.

Certainly, you can learn vocal production, but it's not essential when the basic sound is satisfactory. Actors and singers need special training in vocal production and control; so do people with vocal problems. If you produce sound incorrectly and tend to get hoarse after speaking for a while; if your voice is strident, shrill, and harsh; or if it is excessively nasal or whiney, then you should seek professional help in the production of sound. But barring a real problem, your voice will respond as it should and be pleasant to hear if your face and body are open as you speak.

THE VOCAL TOOLS

There are three vocal tools that you should always be aware of as you speak:

> Volume
> Pitch
> Rate

Volume is the decibel level of the sound: the loudness or softness of your voice.

Pitch is the position of the sound on the musical scale: the highness or lowness of your voice.

Rate is the duration of the sound: the length of time it takes you to make it.

In stress, the muscles of the head and neck tighten and most sounds that are emitted tend to come out the same. That is, every sound seems to take on the same volume, pitch, and rate, which is the definition of monotonous. When your face is closed and you say, "He made an amazing recovery," every syllable sounds just like every other syllable. You're inviting a person listening to you to tune you out, or worse, to misunderstand you. When you open your face, chances are the words will come out something like this:

        AZ

    AM   ING recovery.

He made an

There's variety in the volume and pitch of your voice in that sentence. There's honesty in that sentence.

Volume is the most overused and least effective of the three vocal tools. Years ago, when microphones weren't commonplace, trained, sonorous voices were the norm. Singers, actors, and especially political speakers had to reach the back of huge auditoriums with their own vocal equipment. But as the technical equipment improved, the ability (or lack of ability) of most speakers remained in the 1920s.

The advent of the microphone should have altered speaking styles *drastically* but it hasn't. Before the microphone, it was never possible to speak in an entirely conversational voice and be heard by a large number of people. Now it is. But most inexperienced speakers still tend to speak too loudly in public situations. They approach the microphone, clear their throats, place their voices too far back in their throats (to achieve an air of authority), and speak too loudly—and the sound that comes out is pompous. It's the sound of the great "Ahem," a phony voice, "a platform voice." Yet many of us incorrectly use it, thinking that it's the proper public speaking voice for the serious professional. Young men and women moving up in the business world must be especially careful of this trap. It's very easy to fall into, because they've been led to believe that it's what's expected in the upwardly mobile world. It's not.

One young man, seeing a replay of his before-and-after TV training appearances in a seminar said, "Now I know what you mean. You're telling me to use my living-room voice all the time—not my radio voice." That's it exactly! He said it better than I had. Get rid of the artificial person you think you're supposed to be. Become the person you really are. When in doubt, speak even more quietly. You need only enough volume to be heard. Emphasis and energy should be added by using pitch and rate change rather than by adding volume.

If Ronald Reagan has one distinguishing communication characteristic that makes him excel among political leaders—that makes him almost unique—it is his quiet, warm, convincing, believable, friendly vocal tone. You've almost never heard him speak loudly. If he has a short temper and raises his voice, it's almost always done in complete privacy. Only his closest aides have come to see that side of him. In public, before a microphone, even when he is addressing a huge audience, he uses the quiet tones of everyday conversation.

Try saying these sentences with no expression:

She's a remarkable person.
It was a delightful show.
He's a dynamite speaker.
You believed that liar?
It was an overpowering experience.
He's never done an honest day's work in his life.
Just who does she think she is?

Now open your face and your body and use the three vocal tools—volume, pitch, and rate—to *really* make these sentences mean what you want them to mean. It makes a big difference, doesn't it?

▪ VOCAL STYLE

When you're called upon to speak, watch out for the *toos*. You don't want your volume too loud or too soft. You don't want your pitch too high or too low. You don't want your rate too fast or too slow.

When you open your face and your body, you produce a warm conversational sound, probably the most pleasant sound you're capable of. You're being yourself.

So your speaking style involves coordinated and proper use of the face, body, and voice—all of which combine to get your message across to your audience. When they're working together and correctly, an audience hears and understands your message. It needs only to be present and attentive—it needs to do no work, to make no effort.

And that point leads me to another. I believe that if everyone in the world could learn to communicate effectively, we wouldn't need courses in effective listening techniques. We need to develop listening skills because the people we listen to aren't communicating. Most of the people we listen to are dull. They aren't giving. They aren't sharing. They aren't *loving*. So we have to do the work for them. For communication to be perfect, the audience should be required to do nothing—just show up and be willing to be attentive. Only then can communication be complete. Only then can the audience truly receive your ideas. They don't need to cut through a lot of dullness, a lot of personal idiosyncrasies, a lot of garbage. The communication is made. It's shared. An act of love has taken place on an intellectual level.

▪ THE TELEPHONE

The telephone is one of the blessings and curses of the twentieth century. Without it, we'd be lost. With it, we've become addicted.

Most executives spend an enormous amount of time on the phone, and secretaries, receptionists, and assistants often spend even more time on the telephone than the boss. Even our social hours find us "reaching out" a lot. And most of us never give a second thought—or even a first thought—to what comes over the earpiece to the person on the other end.

After you've said "Hello" has anyone ever said to you, "Did I wake you?" "Do you feel OK?" "Is anything wrong?" or "What's the matter?" If so, your voice obviously sent a sick, bored, worried, or tired signal. You didn't make the necessary effort.

You need to take the phone seriously as a communication tool. You have to make a good impression. The obvious, usually overlooked fact is that the telephone is often the first and sometimes the only contact we have with the person on the other end of the line. You don't want that person turned off by a tired voice, by a bored voice, by a monotonous voice. And most of all, you don't want him turned off by a rude voice. Obviously, you want a happy, pleasant, warm, friendly voice representing you, just as you want to hear those same qualities when you call someone.

It amazes me that corporations that spend vast sums on training, meetings, and conventions ignore the telephone communication skills of the receptionist, the secretary, and the executive. One company always asks me to work with all its telephone-answering personnel at the end of each session. On a recent return visit, one of the receptionists I had trained at the previous program thanked me. She said that since she had learned how to brighten up her telephone delivery she had received three promotions. It really works.

Even though the voice is the only communication tool that makes it through the mouthpiece, don't forget the face and the body. Although the person on the other end of the line can't see them, remember that your voice *follows* your face and your body. If you work at opening your face and punctuating important points with gestures, your voice will begin to open up. On the phone, as in a radio interview, it's also important to give variety to the pitch and rate movement of your voice.

A public relations assistant told me, "When I give telephone interviews to reporters, I remember to open my face and to gesture so my voice will register warmth, willingness to cooperate, and honesty. And you know what? They seem to be more interested in what I'm saying. I'm being quoted more accurately, and the articles have been more favorable. Nothing beats having the reporter trust you to be telling the truth. My only regret is that we didn't do this twenty years ago."

A closed-face "Good morning" over the telephone isn't a good morning at all. In fact, it's a rotten morning. An open-faced "Good morning" is a genuine greeting. You'll be spending a lot of the rest of your life on the phone, so make it pay off for you. Put your face and your body into your phone and delight your listener.

WINNING

WITH SKILL: USING YOUR MIND

What usually happens to most of us when a still photographer yells, "Hold it"? We simply don't know *what to do* at that moment. We tense up immediately. We think, "Is my hair neat?" Men proceed to do a Rodney Dangerfield tug at the tie or check to make sure the fly is zipped. Women straighten the skirt. Or we tighten the muscles from the shoulders up to make sure we're standing erect. We force a smile. We pose. We concentrate on all the wrong things. We become robots. Our minds have failed us.

When I said that style is as important as substance in any speaking situation, I certainly wasn't trying to diminish the importance of your mind. After all, if you have nothing to say but deliver well, you won't get very far if your audience discovers that truth. I believe that if the audience doesn't like the way you look and the way you sound, they'll never discover your mind. But you also have to use your mind to control the way you look and sound and give real meaning to what you say.

An actor may recite his lines perfectly. His voice is just right, he's got all his gestures down pat. But he still gives a lousy performance. Why? Because he isn't using his mind.

Your mind is your substance. It's what you know. It's the battery that makes the whole machine work. Don't sell it short, and don't let anyone cause you to let it malfunction. It's your mind that allows your style to come through and demonstrate your uniqueness. No one else has exactly your body of knowledge. No one else brings precisely your perspective to information. In other words, your mind is just as important as your face, your body, and your voice in every speaking situation. My point can be summed up in a very familiar phrase—think before you speak.

▪ PREPARE

In a normal speaking situation, the key to using your mind properly is preparation. Obviously, if you don't have anything to say, don't say anything. If you don't know anything about a certain subject, listen and learn something. Yes, some people are better than others at thinking on their feet. But very few memorable sayings were impromptu utterances. Hardly any quotable statements were spontaneous. Most of the great one-liners of comedy were carefully crafted and rehearsed so that in delivery they'd seem spontaneous, and the timing of the delivery would be perfect.

The singer prepares constantly, concentrating on perfecting skills and techniques. The concert musician concentrates on perfecting his or her craft and practices endlessly. The speaker needn't devote a lifetime to developing his or her skills, but drafting, editing, and rehearsing material *and* delivery does require concentration, time, and mental agility. And whatever the situation, the goals of all your mental efforts should be to:

Be prepared	Be comfortable
Be concise	Be communicative
Be clear	Be yourself
Be confident	

All speaking, all oral communication, should be based on conversation. So my first rule is, Don't ever make a speech. Talk to your audience. Have a conversation with a group of people.

THE DON'TS	THE DOS
Don't preach	Converse
Don't orate	Chat
Don't teach	Talk
Don't deliver a speech, a sermon, a lecture, or a lesson	Make the setting your living room rather than an auditorium
	Confide in your audience
	Tell an interesting story
	Treat an audience exactly as you would a single listener

Remember the earlier point that communication is the transfer of ideas from the mind of the communicator to the minds of the audience. It's a sharing of information and an intellectual act of love. I *want* you to understand what I'm saying. I *want* you to receive my message. I *want* you to remember my ideas. So I'm going to do everything I can to get my information across to you. I'm going to be enthusiastic about my information, energetic, interested in you, and interesting for you to see and to hear.

Think about the classroom for a minute. Teachers have traditionally been selected on the basis of education and background. Both are very important. But in reality teachers should also be chosen on the basis of their *ability to communicate*. It sounds revolutionary, and maybe it is. But the person with the greatest mind in the world may prove to be a terrible teacher, and one with a mediocre mind may be a great teacher. The difference is the ability of each to get across the subject to the students, the listeners.

GET YOUR ACT TOGETHER

If you're going to talk, you'd better know what you're going to talk about. You've got to be the authority. You have to possess information worth sharing, or else why get up in the first place? Obviously, preparation is the key.

Most of us don't spend enough time getting ready for a speaking assignment. If we do spend a lot of hours, many if not most of them are wasted. It's a pity that we rarely do the right things to get ready to give a presentation to an audience. We worry a lot, we make a lot of false starts, we go through a lot of self-doubt and agony—all time wasters and counterproductive. So let's consider what the right things are. Everything is governed by what you're going to say and how you're going to say it.

What you talk about is almost totally dependent on your audience, the circumstances surrounding your appearance, and, naturally, the ground rules. For example, the person asking you to speak may request that you talk for forty-five minutes about the effects of a bill before Congress changing the current tax law. You may be asked to give a report on the financial situation of your company or association to the board of directors. You may be expected to read the minutes you took of the last meeting of the civic group you belong to. You may be headed for the school board meeting that has under consideration closing your neighborhood school. You know you want to be heard on this issue. You're well advised in each of these scenarios and just about every other to be well prepared, to plan your remarks beforehand.

WRITE BEFORE YOU SPEAK

There are several ways to prepare to deliver your speech or presentation. Of course you can use a manuscript or choose an outline. Some people work best using notes. Still others prefer to bring nothing with them to the lectern. It's completely a matter of personal choice, and I recommend using what works best for you. But I suggest beginning with a prepared text, an actual manuscript. By preparing the script, you'll have taken the time to structure your remarks. Since reading from a manuscript is the hardest kind of speech to deliver well, we'll talk about the techniques of delivery when you have a manuscript in front of you. My principle is that if you can handle the most difficult scenario, you'll be able to handle any situation.

In preparing your script, print or use a typewriter with large type. The larger the type, the easier it is to see the words. Leave an extra-wide left-hand margin. That will mean fewer words per line. Separate your pages; remove the staple, paper clip, or whatever else you used to fasten them. Now you'll be able to slide pages rather than turn them. You really don't want your audience to be counting your pages, and that's what they'll be doing if they watch each page being turned. They'll also start wondering how many more you have to go. As you slide page one over, leave it alone. Don't put it under the rest of the text. When you're finished your pages will be in reverse order, but you're finished. They don't need to be in proper order. And later you'll have all the time in the world to put them back in proper order.

Number your pages in the upper right-hand corner. That way, as soon as you begin to slide page one from right to left you'll have the comforting knowledge that page two is right where it belongs. If you see page seven instead of page two, you know you're in trouble. STOP. Tell the audience your pages got mixed up. Straighten out the mess before their very eyes. An audience loves this kind of honesty and certainly prefers it to inept groping while trying to continue. But really, your pages shouldn't be out of order. After all, you're the last person to handle the text and it's something you should check just before you approach the lectern.

Don't type all the way down to the bottom of the page. Leave at least a one-inch margin at the bottom. Leave even more blank space at the bottom if possible. Then, when you do look down to check your text, you won't be showing us the top of your head. In fact, if the microphone position permits, take a half step back from the lectern and now you'll be able to see the bottom lines by glancing down instead of having to lower your chin down to your chest. When you stand flush up against the lectern and look down toward the bottom line of text, it looks as though you're checking your navel. It leaves a lot to be desired.

Everything on the right side of the page should be neatly typed. Everything in the wide left-hand margin should be written in your own hand. In the upper left-hand corner of every page, draw for yourself a reminder of what you want to do. Draw a happy open face. It's hard to look down, see the face, and not open up. If you tend to be too loud at the lectern, as most of us do, write under the face the admonition "Shhhhh!"

Your finished manuscript should look like the one on page

44. Let's assume that book page is your 8½-by-11-inch sheet of paper. That's the look of the text. Now for the text itself.

▪BE CONCISE

A lot of us have what I call intellectual dysentery. If we get a thought, it's got to come pouring out. That's very destructive at the podium. The audience wants, needs, and deserves organization—a well-developed idea, clearly and precisely presented. It's your job as the speaker to remove the garbage, the extraneous thoughts from the speech. It's impossible to tell an audience everything you know about a given subject. Even more important, they don't want to hear everything you know. They want you to be selective. They want you to tell them what they need to know to be informed.

For all the complaints about the "shallowness" of television news coverage, it's exactly what the public seems to want. Very few people read the entire text of *The New York Times,* or *The Washington Post,* or the *Los Angeles Times* or the *St. Louis Post-Dispatch.* They read about what interests them. Television news is even more limited, and we've come to expect our TV news teams to give us a dynamic, highly selective series of stories that will prove interesting to most viewers. They do that with great skill. People who want more than the networks or their local stations provide turn to the alternatives: a cable news network, newspapers, in-depth studies done in other news formats, or weekly magazines.

You need to become the "nightly news" of speakers: dynamic, with well-prepared, meticulously selected material.

▪BE CLEAR

Write conversational English. Most of us, without realizing it, write for posterity; we try to write great literature. Don't. From

SH!!!!
SMILE!
APPROPRIATE
GESTURES
when the
audience sees
me turning pages
they start
COUNTING...

FIRST, USE LARGE TYPE.

THE LARGER THE TYPE, THE EASIER IT IS TO SEE.

LEAVE AN EXTRA-WIDE LEFT-HAND MARGIN.

DOUBLE SPACE THE TEXT.

TRIPLE SPACE PARAGRAPHS.

SEPARATE YOUR PAGES.

REMOVE STAPLES AND PAPER CLIPS.

SLIDE PAGES. DON'T TURN THEM.

LEAVE A ONE OR TWO INCH MARGIN AT THE BOTTOM OF THE PAGE.

THIS SIDE OF THE PAGE SHOULD BE NEATLY TYPED.

USE LEFT-HAND MARGIN FOR HANDWRITTEN NOTES AND THE OPEN FACE.

DON'T START A NEW SENTENCE ON THIS PAGE UNLESS YOU CAN FINISH IT.

EVERY PAGE SHOULD END WITH A PERIOD.

now on, your goal for speaking should be to use basic, simple, clear, understandable language. My basic rule is No sentence should cover more than two lines of type. (And remember, we're now talking about much narrower lines with a wide left-hand margin.) A sentence like

"It is incumbent upon us to ensure that the principles outlined and espoused in the manual of management procedures be adhered to and implemented."

might read

"We've got to follow the manual."

At a platform-speaking workshop I conducted recently, one of the participants used a sentence that consisted of 101 words. Imagine trying to deliver a sentence that long and expect an audience to follow it. A short, snappy sentence is easy to understand. It's easy to remember. It's easy to deliver well. Your speech is delivered for your audience, not for posterity; it won't be read in the twenty-first century. And if it were, its message would probably be appreciated more if we strove for clarity rather than literary immortality. You help yourself tremendously if your text sounds as if you are talking rather than writing for the time capsule.

You may chuckle at the thought of someone delivering a 101-word sentence, but take a look at an old speech of yours, or look at a book of speeches or a back issue of the *Congressional Record*. Very few speakers have mastered the techniques of simplicity, clarity, and brevity.

Here's an excerpt from a piece of testimony that was delivered to the Subcommittee on Roads of the Committee on Public Works of the U.S. House of Representatives:

In the face of these circumstances for the Congress to have appropriated only $80 million for fiscal year 1972 and for the budget to request only $90 million for fiscal year 1973 for State and community programs is, in our judgment, un-reality bordering on irresponsibility—particularly in the face of more mileage, more cars, more drivers, and more deaths, and injuries on the highways.

This sentence was ostensibly written to be spoken aloud. It contains sixty-six words (if you substitute the word *dollars* for the two dollar signs), there are six commas and a dash.

For delivery, I'd suggest the speaker change the text to read something like this:

> There are more cars on the road than ever before. There are more drivers. More miles are being logged every year. And more innocent people are being killed and maimed. And Congress has only appropriated $80 million for fiscal 1972 and $90 million for 1973. It's unreal. It borders on being downright irresponsible.

My version may not be perfect, but it's a darn sight more readable. And that makes it a lot more interesting for an audience to listen to if it's spoken well.

Consider two more examples. Harry Truman and Douglas MacArthur each had many admirers, but they became adversaries during Truman's presidency. And each was capable of quotable, memorable speech, like Truman's "The buck stops here" and MacArthur's "I shall return." I don't want you to think for one second that I'm making a political judgment when I say that generally Truman was more concerned with the clarity and directness of his discourse in formal speech and that MacArthur was writing for posterity.

Here are some excerpts from Harry Truman's State of the Union Address in 1951:

The United States and the whole free world are passing through a period of grave danger. Every action you take here in Congress and every action I take as President must be measured against the test of whether it helps to meet that danger.

This will be a presidential election year—the year in which politics plays a large part in our lives—a larger part than usual. That's perfectly proper. But we have a great responsibility to conduct our political fights in a manner that does not hurt our national interest.

We can find plenty of things to differ about without destroying our free institutions and without abandoning our bipartisan foreign policy for peace.

When everything is said and done, all of us—Republicans and Democrats alike—all of us are Americans, and we are all going to sink or swim together.

. . . At the present session of the United Nations in Paris, we, together with the British and the French, offered a plan to reduce and control all armaments under a foolproof inspection system. This is a concrete, practical proposal for disarmament.

But what happened? Vishinsky laughed at it. Listen to what he said: "I could hardly sleep at all last night—I could not sleep because I kept laughing." The world will be a long time forgetting the spectacle of that fellow laughing at disarmament.

Disarmament is not a joke. Vishinsky's laughter met with shock and anger from people all over the world. And, as a result, Mr. Stalin's representative received orders to stop laughing and start talking.

Truman's sentences are generally short and to the point. His paragraphs are short and concise. The text is highly readable and certainly memorable. Contrast his words with those delivered by Douglas MacArthur to the Congress:

> I stand on this rostrum with a sense of deep humility and pride—humility in the weight of those great architects of our history who have stood here before me, pride in the reflection that this home of legislative debate represents human liberty in the purest form yet devised.
>   . . . Long exploited by the so-called colonial powers, with little opportunity to achieve any degree of social justice, individual dignity, or a higher standard of life such as guided our own noble administration in the Philippines, the people of Asia found their opportunity in the war just past to throw off the shackles of colonialism and now see the dawn of new opportunity, and heretofore unfelt dignity, and the self-respect of political freedom.
>   Mustering half of the earth's population, and 60 percent of its natural resources, these peoples are rapidly consolidating a new force, both moral and material, with which to raise the living standard and erect adaptations of the design of modern progress to their own distinct cultural environments.

The first MacArthur paragraph is 49 words in a single sentence. The second is 74 words, and again a single sentence. The third is 47 words and one sentence. And I doubt that you remember what he said in any one of those paragraphs on first reading.

Truman was writing for an immediate impact. MacArthur was attempting great literature. Truman's speech was the more successful, in my opinion, because conversation is the key element of all spoken communication. And literature rarely makes good speech material.

I'm not anti-eloquence. I'm anti-unspeakable text. Writing for the eye is different from writing for the ear. A good speech reads well. Not all literature makes a good speech.

Winston Churchill also had a tendency to overblown speech. But when it really counted, he could come straight to the point. As Great Britain was fighting for its life during World War II before America's entry into the war, Churchill wrote to President Roosevelt, "Send us the tools and we will do the job."

That's ten words. They say it all.

Give that same request to an American bureaucrat and it probably would have read something like this:

"If it is deemed appropriate and desirable by your government to cooperate with the efforts and military goals of our government, it would be appreciated with gratitude if your government would expeditiously acquiesce and dispatch to our government the tools and implements necessary for us to continue our effort to vanquish our mutual enemy in a propitious manner."

If you've seen it once, you've seen it a hundred times from a hundred different sources:

- The Lord's Prayer contains 56 words.
- The Twenty-third Psalm, 118 words.
- The Gettysburg Address, 226 words.
- The Ten Commandments, 297 words.
- An old Department of Agriculture regulation on red cabbage, 15,629 words.

So, first edit yourself. Get rid of the pompous tendency to show off. Instead of trying to impress your audience with your knowledge, impress them with the clarity of your expression. Get rid of literary words and start substituting conversational words. Here are some perfectly good words and expressions to *avoid* when you're speaking:

Thus	As it were
However	In a manner of speaking
Nevertheless	Whereas
Hence	Per se
Heretofore	Quid pro quo
Moreover	Perhaps
Therefore	Promulgate
Ergo	Prioritize
If you will	Parameters
If I may	Alas

And the list goes on. You should be able to add a couple of dozen of your own favorites.

My own favorite is *indeed*. It's a truly literary word. It means "what I'm about to say should be emphasized." It never needs to be spoken. Instead, the speaker should deliver what follows more emphatically, more dramatically, and eliminate the word *indeed* from the spoken delivery. Notice how many journalists use the word. It's an excellent way to show emphasis in written material, but it's terrible when spoken. Still, too many people use it in speech because no one ever told them it makes them sound pompous. Even President Reagan's speech writers have given him a lot of unnecessary *indeeds*. And even he can't make them sound natural, because they aren't.

Here's another sentence that may help you picture the difference between literary and conversational words even more clearly: "I urge you to interface, replicate, and exacerbate only in the privacy of your own home." There is no place for words like these in the speaker's vocabulary.

And speaking of getting rid of things, how about acronyms and abbreviations? They're absolutely acceptable when everyone in your audience knows what they mean. But offer the added courtesy of saying the full name first and then follow it immediately with the acronym or abbreviation. After that, the acronym or the abbreviation alone will do. I'm thinking of the less obvious ones like N.I.O.S.H., the C.P.S.C., or T.S.C.A. Maybe everyone now knows the EPA, but not everyone knows the first three.

My point is this: There's nothing wrong with the acronyms or the words on my literary word list. But since we don't use them in casual conversation, they tend to make an audience aware of our language rather than of our ideas. They start to worry about us being pompous. They may not even realize it, but they tend to tune us out.

The Washington Word Game that pops up from time to time in newspapers and magazines makes my point for me. You're to select one word from each of three columns and put together a perfectly governmentese phrase. The more words you use, the less likely you are to say anything meaningful but manage to sound important. Try any combination of one word from each column.

WASHINGTON WORD GAME

COLUMN A	COLUMN B	COLUMN C
indigenous	environmental	overkill
comprehensive	neutral	pollution
fragmentary	concomitant	interface
interplanetary	philosophical	replication
internecine	totalitarian	exacerbation
collective	demagogic	dialectic
bureaucratic	proactive	evaluation
portentous	demonstrative	resonance
didactic	hedonistic	fallacy
pedantic	antediluvian	methodology
ultimate	gustatory	phalanx
incorrigible	dyslexic	retrogression
corporeal	pragmatic	monasticism

Anyone can play. It's fun.

WINNING

WITH

CONFIDENCE

Your message is prepared correctly on the page. The type is large and easy to read. The sentences are short, conversational, and snappy. The language is concise. Now we're ready to talk about delivering the message with confidence. And nothing is more important to your delivery than the way you breathe.

ᴮBREATHING FOR LIFE

There are other benefits from learning proper breathing techniques. People who breathe correctly in stressful situations rarely die of a sudden heart attack or stroke while in their fifties and sixties. Think about it. Trained singers, stage actors, wind and reed musicians, and athletes are generally taught the proper way to breathe early in their careers. In fact, a good vocal coach never lets a student make the first musical sound until the correct breathing technique is so well learned that it has become part of the singer's normal habit. You'll never see Pavarotti or Domingo or Sutherland breathe an incorrect breath. You won't see Olivier or Gielgud breathe the wrong way.

Correct breathing is the key to metabolic comfort. It's the key to reducing stress naturally, better than any pill ever manufactured. I'm amazed that the health care profession has never gone on a campaign to teach you what I'm going to teach you here. Proper breathing helps reduce the tensions caused by stress— blood pressure tends to normalize, pulse rate tends to get closer to the normal beat. This is because proper breathing enforces us to relax. It's our greatest normalizer. That's why it's the technique taught by the natural childbirth methodologies. It's the method used by yoga and meditation teachers to help you unwind, relax, and cleanse your mind of its unwanted garbage. It helps you achieve a state as close to physical, mental, and emotional freedom as you can.

So breathing is not just a speaking tool, it's a health tool. It's a longevity tool, too. Now, I'm not claiming it's a cure for anything, I'm only saying it can help prevent stress-related problems. But that's saying a lot. And remember, one of the most stressful experiences today is speaking in public.

THE DIAPHRAGM

To learn proper breathing techniques, you first need to know that the center of the breathing mechanism, the main muscle, is the diaphragm, a dome-shaped arch located just under the rib cage, right below the breastbone. The lungs rest on the diaphragm, so when you look for your diaphragm, if you find yourself anywhere near your navel, you're too far south.

The proper breathing rhythm is for the diaphragm to flatten on inhalation. On exhalation the diaphragm returns to its arched position and actually forces air out of the lungs by pushing upward. Place your fingers against your diaphragm. On an inhalation, your fingers should be forced away from your body. On the exhalation, your fingers should move back toward your body. Remember, many people do it wrong. Often, when we think about breathing, we suck the diaphragm in when we inhale. Don't. This comes from military training, posture training, and an involuntary reaction to stress or fear. It goes back to that terrible notion of sucking in your gut. It's not only wrong, it's self-defeating.

Look at yourself in the mirror. Pretend the doctor has just told you to take a deep breath. If you're pulling in on your diaphragm, your shoulders are heaving upward. It's exactly the wrong thing to do. Your shoulders shouldn't move on inhalation. The lungs need room to expand, and the movement all should be outward not upward. Yawning and sighing are almost always examples of correct breathing. You always breathe correctly when you're lying on your back as you fall asleep. The trouble is that you can't check on your breathing while you sleep. But for a real test, lie down on your back. Fold your arms over your diaphragm and close your eyes. Notice that by the third or fourth breath your rhythm is normal and correct. Your diaphragm is moving away from your spine on inhalation and back toward the spine as you exhale.

YOU LOSE when you breathe incorrectly. Correct breathing is the key to relaxation. You control your body rather than your body controlling you.

It's harder to accomplish this rhythm when you're standing, so try standing up. Place your fingers on your diaphragm. Take a gentle but forceful breath. Don't breathe deeply but breathe physically. Push your fingers away from your body as you inhale. Now exhale and let your fingers return toward your body. Inhale again, making a forceful movement outward on your fingers. Return your fingers toward your body on the exhalation. Try this three or four times. Now close your eyes and repeat it several more times. Notice what a surge of well-being now flows through your body. Your metabolism is normalizing, relaxing, moving toward peace. This is the state that hypnotherapists try to induce prior to the hypnotic state. As I mentioned, it's the proper state in which to achieve yoga and meditation.

As another exercise, press the fingers of one hand into the diaphragm. Place the fingers of the other hand on the back of your neck. Make a conscious effort to breathe wrong. Suck your

diaphragm in as you inhale. Notice how tense the muscles in the back of your neck have become. Your whole head is filling with tension; actually, so is your whole body. Now do the same thing with both hands, but force yourself to breathe correctly. Let your breath move your fingers gently away from your body as you breathe in. Exhale. Do it again. Push your fingers slightly and gently away as you take in another breath. Exhale. Feel the tension race out of the back of your neck. You're experiencing the first leg of your journey toward relaxation.

In perhaps three or four breaths, you have your body reacting the way you want it to rather than to the stress of a given situation. You are controlling your body rather than letting your body control you.

Obviously, you can't stand up in front of your board of directors, smile, and say, "Hold it just a second, folks," then go into your breathing exercises. But you certainly can practice proper breathing techniques inconspicuously while waiting your turn to speak. You can practice correct breathing anytime you're alone or anytime you're in a group when the group is attentive to someone else. In fact, once you've mastered the technique, you can do it anywhere, anytime. If it's done correctly, it doesn't require special finger placement and is totally inconspicuous. Now your mind can take over.

I also like to recommend practicing proper breathing on the telephone. Most of us spend a tremendous amount of time on the phone. It's a great time to put your free hand on the diaphragm and "make it happen." It won't be long before you're breathing correctly all the time.

But when stress strikes, all bets are off. Just about everyone tends to tighten their muscles and breathe wrong when the boom is lowered.

- You're furious because one of your colleagues just single-handedly lost your biggest client with a stupid, thoughtless, avoidable act.
- One of your children just totaled your car in a truly careless accident. He's OK—no injury, but now all you can think of is the stupidity of the act.
- Your mayor just announced that the city is doubling your real estate taxes.
- You're in a meeting with the top brass of your department. The department manager is just concluding the opening remarks and you know that in a matter of seconds it will be your turn to speak . . .

In situations like these, stop. Take several gentle diaphragmatic breaths. Let your breathing help you get hold of yourself. Let your breathing force the tension out of your body and soothe you back into comfort and control.

The problem, of course, is realizing that you're in a stressful state when you're in it. Usually, extreme stress is so extreme that it takes over and we are unaware of anything else. It's vitally important that you be able to learn how to recognize when you're in stress. Otherwise, you won't be able to control it because you won't have the presence of mind to concentrate on letting your breathing release you from the prison of stress. I know it's difficult to concentrate on a physical subject like breathing when you're being emotionally crucified, but the more you let panic reign, the harder it is to throw it off. Once again, breathing is basic, it's fundamental. Good oral communication begins with good breathing. Self-control is the name of the game.

If you suffer the pangs of fear and stress when you know you're going to speak, listen to two of the people I trained who were just like you:

"When I feel a panic attack coming on, I stop, take two or three diaphragmatic breaths, and I'm back in command of myself and my situation."

"I'm convinced that breathing is the most important lesson I got. I'm much more in control of myself. It really amazes me to be able to be confident in what used to be a bad situation."

Even the most experienced speakers have told me that proper breathing before—and *during*—their presentations is a vital ingredient in delivering their message with confidence. And when you have self-confidence, your audience will have confidence in you.

SENDING
WINNING
SIGNALS

Now you're relaxed. And what's more important, you now know how to use proper breathing techniques to help you stay relaxed. Your text is prepared for comfortable, dynamic delivery. And you've become familiar with your material, you've made it your own. The next step is to learn how to send winning signals, the signals that will make your audience like you and believe what you say. We've all heard about body language. We know about nonverbal communication. Sending winning signals includes these and more.

The way you breathe sends signals. If your shoulders heave as you inhale, you look tight, stiff, intimidated. You may not be aware of it while it's happening, but your audience will read those signals and think you're uncomfortable. If it goes on long enough, you'll eventually make your audience uncomfortable, too.

The way you use your face, your hands, and your voice sends signals. What you wear sends signals. So does your general appearance, your grooming. In short, as long as your audience can see you, what is seen is just as important as what you say.

In any speaking situation, it's your job to make sure the audience can receive the message you intend to send. This is not as simple as it sounds. It means that you must appear to be both comfortable and in control whether you're standing behind a lectern or sitting at a conference table.

One position most people find uncomfortable is standing with their hands at their sides. Interestingly, this is the most comfortable position for an audience to look at. It sends the most friendly, open, personable signals. However, most of us try, instead, to hide our hands in some way. By giving in to this impulse, we invariably wind up in an awkward, if not embarrassing, position. Most men go right for the fig leaf, most women fold their arms in front of them. Some people thrust their hands in their pockets, while others try to hide their hands behind their backs. None of these stances looks comfortable or inviting to an audience. Worst of all, they all send signals that usually will be interpreted correctly by an audience as signs of stiffness or insecurity. Yet, time after time, people automatically assume one of these hand-hiding positions.

You can see examples of this for yourself by looking at photographs of award ceremonies, company meetings, even social functions. At the summit meetings in Switzerland in 1985, Iceland in 1986, and Washington in 1987, President Reagan and Chairman Gorbachev were usually seen with their hands comfortably at their sides. Here were the leaders of the two most powerful nations in the world looking perfectly at ease with each other. It almost seemed like a contest to see who could appear more relaxed. Yet, in the background were all their aides, in the familiar fig-leaf or folded-arm positions, or in a stiff, military, hands-behind-back pose. It was almost comical.

What *you* can learn from this is how to send the signals that show your audience that you are comfortable and in control.

How to stand

When you are standing, I recommend this position:

- Erect posture
- Feet about shoulder-width apart
- One foot slightly in front of the other
- Hands comfortably resting at your sides
- Head erect
- Chin up but not exaggerated

Here are the messages you'll send in this position:

- An erect posture suggests authority.
- Feet spread suggests solidity.
- One foot slightly forward lets you move toward your audience as you gesture. It suggests the embrace and hug I spoke of earlier.
- With your hands at your sides, you look natural and comfortable.
- Keeping your head erect with chin up prevents you from look-

ing down at your audience—or worse, from looking down your
nose at your audience—or from tilting your head to one side.

I've noticed that many women stand with their heads tilted
to one side. It weakens the communication. Your head should
be erect and still. I say still because many of us react with our
heads as we listen. We nod while people are talking to us. The
nod means, "I understand what you're telling me," but too often
the things we nod about are negative and it looks as though we
agree. For example, I see a lot of people nod unwittingly as they're
being accused of wrongdoing. That can look very bad.

Once you're comfortable with this standing position, take a
couple of diaphragmatic breaths. Then, shake out your shoulders
and see where your hands fall naturally. They should now be at
your sides. Fingers that fidget, clutch at things, or are fully ex-
tended won't look comfortable to an audience. So avoid the
temptation to wiggle your fingers or tug at your clothing. Your
fingers should be curled slightly, with the thumb toward your
audience. Don't let your palm or the back of your hand face out.

Naturally, I don't recommend that you stand like a statue.
Use gestures to punctuate what you're saying. After the first few
gestures, you'll find that your hands can come to lots of other
positions. For example, your fingers could be folded comfortably
in front of the waist; one hand could be in a pocket, the other
at your side; or both hands could be in pockets.

Whatever subsequent positions you choose, remember that
the gesture is one of the strongest signals you can send. Like the
open face, it says, "I care about you," "This communication is
important to me," "I hug you with my ideas." Continue to use
your arms and hands in genuine and appropriate gestures at the
appropriate times. Don't succumb to the temptation to hide them.
You'll also find that by varying the hand you use for gestures,
you'll be helping yourself vary the gestures you use.

These same principles apply to the lectern. You can hold the lectern with both hands, but don't clutch it. Clutching the lectern is the podium equivalent of the fig-leaf position. Use the lectern but not as a crutch. Don't become dependent on it to hold you up. And, even standing behind a lectern, use natural and appropriate gestures. A good gesture helps you pump up your energy. It helps you look like you're reaching out to embrace your audience.

▪How to sit

Sitting is usually an easier communication position than standing, but it can be more tricky and deceptive. That's because we're likely to *feel* more comfortable when we're seated but *look* less comfortable. We like to sit back for comfort. We often allow ourselves to "sink in." Sofas and easy chairs, especially, tend to trap us. When we lean back, sink in, or swivel, we appear to lose interest in the person we're talking to or the person who's talking to us. Watch someone who is leaning back. You get the signal that he or she is uninterested in the proceedings.

An exaggerated example of someone who sends the wrong signals is William F. Buckley. He leans so far back in his chair that he seems completely uninterested in the person sharing his program with him. We get the impression of an inflated ego. To add to that impression, his head is often cocked to one side and he literally looks down his nose at his guest.

If you lean back in your chair, you're probably sending the signal that you don't care very much about what you're saying or whoever is listening to you. When you're alone or surrounded by people you know well, any position is fine. But when you're trying to make a favorable impression or when an audience is looking at you, I recommend these tactics:

- Sit with your spine erect but not exaggerated.
- Lean slightly forward.

YOU WIN in informal speaking situations when you sit up straight, keep your spine away from the back of the chair, and are not afraid to gesture.

- Keep your knees together.
- If you cross your legs, cross the overleg at a downward angle. The least attractive part of your wardrobe is the sole of your shoe. So why put it on display?
- Have your hands in a comfortable position and free to gesture.
- Keep your spine away from the back of the chair to resist the temptation to slump.
- If the chair has arms, your arms can rest on them, but don't let your hands dangle. Your hands may touch but must not clutch the chair arms. You can rest your hands on your thighs if you prefer. If you fold your hands, leave them loose to encourage gestures.

Sitting erect and leaning slightly forward as you speak will send the right signals.

˙How to react

Signals are being sent and received even when you're not speaking. Consider all those figures seated at the head table listening (or not listening) to the speaker. Consider the panel members who seem to be rude to the fellow panelists. Consider the picture of the Vice President and the Speaker of the House seated behind the President as he delivers his speech to a joint session of the Congress. And how about the Secret Service personnel and aides in view during a White House press conference?

My point here is that even when you're not speaking, you must learn how to react if the eyes of the audience are on you. And, to be believable, those reactions must be genuine and appropriate. It's as important to a career as learning how to speak well; neither is complete without the other. And here, too, a sure sign of interest, caring, and good attentive listening is the open face.

Now, contrast the previous examples of people listening with the way you're used to seeing Mrs. Reagan as her husband is speaking. She's attentive, interested, respectful. In fact, if any criticism can be leveled, it's that she often appears too adoring.

I don't think I'll ever forget this moment: A friend met me on the street. He was totally surprised to see me. I also think he was quite pleased to see me. His face lit up. His voice literally sang out, "Hi, Arch. It's great to see you again." It was a wonderful greeting. But in the next instant, he remembered that he hadn't been feeling well that morning. He let his eyes narrow, his jaw drop, and his shoulders droop, and said in a mournful voice, "Do I look tired to you?" He certainly did. He sent the exact signals he had meant to send. But were they believable?

Signals can be just as important in one-on-one communication as in group communication. After all, we're usually talking to one other person, not a group. The public, or group, speaking situation is much more rare. Yet, much too often in one-on-one communication, one person tells another, "That's not what you said," or "I don't remember you saying that." In all probability, when this kind of missed communication occurs, the signals were wrong.

This kind of signal sending and receiving touches every facet of our lives. Consider the doctor–patient relationship called bedside manner. Have you ever heard these words: "He's a great doctor, but I get the feeling that he doesn't really care. I'm just another patient to him." He probably really does care. After all, what doctors do is "care" for people. Many are simply unaware of the signals they're sending to their patients or are unaware of how to send the signals that say "I care" other than simply treating the illness.

Think about the signals in the boss–employee relationship and those between colleagues. Think about the signals in the parent–child and teacher–student relationships. And, more often than not, relationship problems are caused by misunderstood signals rather than by misunderstood words.

The words we select, the way we sound, and the way we look all have an important bearing on the signals we send. It doesn't really matter what we say if it doesn't reach the hearer the way we intend.

Clothing

In addition to your face and your posture, your clothes send signals even before you have said a word. The manager in a local bank is out of place in jeans and a baggy sweater. The staff of the regional office of the Department of Agriculture is not to be seen in three-piece suits carrying leather attaché cases. Collars open down to the waist and a neck hung with gold chains won't make it at IBM.

Clothing must be compatible with the situation and the audience. But most important of all is that clothing shouldn't call attention to itself. Nothing you do and nothing you wear should be noticeable in and of itself. Everything about you should be inconspicuous and should blend in except your message. That's what you want your audience to take away with it: your ideas, your mind, your communication.

Mark Twain said, "Clothes make the man. Naked people have little or no influence upon society"—neither do inappropriately dressed people. Clothes should fit well, look comfortable, and be appropriate.

If your clothes fit you well, leave your jacket buttoned when you're standing; seated, leave it unbuttoned. Walter Cronkite and Ronald Reagan are about the only two people I've ever seen who look as if they've had their clothes tailored for the sitting position. Most of us wind up looking like we left the hanger in the jacket when we put in on this morning. When you're seated, a jacket tends to climb up the back of your neck, leaving a gap between the shirt collar and the jacket collar. It looks sloppy. If this hap-

YOU LOSE when you give your audience something else to look at—like crossed legs that expose bare skin.

pens to you, pull the tail of the jacket down as far as it will go and sit on it. That will keep the collar from traveling up.

Bare skin that isn't supposed to be bare is distracting. Bare skin is for the beach. We should never see more skin than we ought to see in a speaking or a professional situation. So, for men, I advise long-sleeved shirts and over-the-calf socks. When short-sleeved shirts are appropriate, it's probably also appropriate to shed the jacket, but a lot of bare arm under a jacket looks underdressed, if not undressed. And the same goes for socks; we don't want to see skin under the trouser leg.

Women should wear blouses buttoned high, at least above the line where the cleavage begins. And in public appearances, no slit skirts or mini-skirts, please. Your audience shouldn't be encouraged to take physical inventory when it should be concentrating on your message. If you suspect the room will be overheated, take off your jacket or sweater before you enter the room. There's something suggestive of a stripper when you dress down in public. The act of removing clothes also highlights the curves of the form, and that always calls attention to itself.

JEWELRY

The same rules apply to jewelry. In purely social situations, almost anything goes. But when you're in the spotlight, your audience shouldn't be aware of your jewelry. Anything that catches its eye (or its ear, for that matter) tends to distract your audience and make it work harder to get your message. Sometimes it can even make your audience oblivious to your message.

Your jewelry should be subdued for a professional or speaking situation. Some women forget this when wearing earrings. Earrings that dangle well below the ear always swing with the slightest head movement. The audience becomes fascinated by the movement and loses sight of what the speaker is saying. Also keep in mind that heavy, expensive-looking, glittery, or ostentatious jewelry may be appropriate at a ball or a fund-raising gala but not on the platform. In general, no audience wants to be aware of how expensively you're bejeweled. It can be a huge turn-off.

A group of people were attending a training session to prepare them to appeal to a foundation for funding. They were looking for a grant of several million dollars, which would be used to help people restore homes in a run-down neighborhood. As a pilot project designed to restore pride, it would be a model program and a truly worthwhile request. The sponsoring organization felt that it would be most effective to have the appeal made by neighborhood residents and business owners instead of bureaucrats. It was a brilliant concept. Who better to tell the story than the real people who were involved, interested, and filled with passion for the project?

As the training progressed, I noticed that one of the resident women was wearing a set of gold bracelets that went from her wrist to her elbow. I suggested that she remove the jewelry for the presentation. She shot me a withering look and said, "These bracelets *never* leave my arm." I honestly believe that it was one of the contributing reasons why the grant was denied. The moral to that story—blatant jewelry displays should be reserved for the people who make it part of their mystique, like Zsa Zsa Gabor and Elizabeth Taylor.

Again, communication means moving what's in your mind directly and easily into the mind of your listener. Anything that gets in the way of the movement, the intellectual movement, tends to destroy communication. The person who is not aware of what you're wearing, how you're standing or sitting, or what you're doing is free to concentrate on your message. All the signals you send should be communication signals not personal signals. Allow your audience to get what you want it to get, what's on your mind.

Ideally, your dress and appearance should be conservative and appropriate to the situation. Conservative means not particularly noticeable. Dress for the occasion but don't overdress.

A classic example of appearance as a signal sender involved two labor union strikes. The contrast deserves pointing out. A few years ago, the Professional Air Traffic Controllers (PATCO) went out on strike. Naturally, every detail of the strike was fodder for the TV cameras. And what did we see? We saw a bunch of relatively young, hippielike, bearded men in cut-off jeans and long-haired women flashing the clenched-fist power salute. They were probably educated, professional human beings. Many men were Viet Nam veterans. Their cause may have been just. They certainly believed in it, but their signals were *wrong*.

More recently United Airlines' pilots went on strike. The TV cameras were there, too, as "We take you now to the airport and the Channel 95 news team . . ." But, this time, we saw meticulously dressed, distinguished-looking, clean-shaven middle-aged people in uniform behaving in a perfectly professional manner. We liked them. Their signals were *right*.

But compare—each group had responsibility for many lives. The controllers had even more lives to worry about than the pilots. Each group lived with stress every minute on the job. The controllers worked forty, fifty, even sixty hours a week under tremendous pressure. The pilots worked maybe forty hours a month. The controllers were on their own. The pilots had at least one other person in the cockpit to share the responsibility. The controllers were averaging about $30,000 a year. The pilots were averaging well over $100,000 annually. The controllers lost their strike; the pilots won. But logic wasn't what influenced our reaction to both groups. It was the signals.

WINNING

WITH
DIRECTNESS
AND
COURTESY

There is one final technique that will always make a difference in every speaking situation—eye contact. The technique makes every member of your audience feel that you are talking *directly* to him or her, not into thin air.

It's remarkable how few speakers use the correct eye contact. It's the most misunderstood concept in public speaking. This may be because so few teachers and trainers know about it. Of course the teleprompter has been a tremendous help to those who have access to it, but most of us have never even seen one, much less had the opportunity to use one.

Formal spoken communication is almost always delivered less interestingly than it should be. We think, "Well, I'm saying real words. My audience is familiar with the words. It isn't as though I'm speaking a foreign language. So if I utter the words they'll get my meaning." Right? Wrong.

Most speakers deliver anywhere from 35 to 85 percent of their speeches to the lectern. Those using a prepared text deliver an even higher percentage of their speech to the text in front of them. So, unless you deliver all of your ideas *directly* to your audience, you might as well *mail them in.*

If you've ever attended a professional meeting where papers were read, you know what I mean. If you've ever paid close attention to politicians droning on endlessly, you know what I mean. If you've ever attended a town council meeting, a school board meeting, or a zoning hearing, you know what I mean. What's missing is direct communication.

As I said before, the fact that we're uttering sounds that are words does not equal communication. Why not? Because communication isn't a one-way street. The act of sending forth words from the mouth of the speaker doesn't mean that the ideas are penetrating the mind of the listener. That's the whole point. Communication means the effortless receipt of the idea by the listener. If I turn my mind "off" while I'm listening to you, communication stops, even though you go on talking.

We've all seen this scenario. The speaker arrives at the lectern. He places his text or notes on the lectern. He glances at the audience. Then he looks down and says, "Good morning." *He says it to the lectern.* Then he glances up to say, "My name is . . ." then his eyes drop down again and *he recites his name to the lectern.* It looks as though he's checking to make sure he remembers his own name. Unfortunately, we all tend to talk to the lectern instead of to our audience. But I've never seen a lectern with ears, have you?

When I'm speaking and you're in my audience, you want to feel that I'm talking to you. When you're speaking and I'm in your audience, I want to feel that you're talking to me. It doesn't matter how large or small the audience. Every single person wants to be part of your talk. They all want to be personally involved with you. And for that to happen, you've got to be personally involved with them. It's this simple, to make them part of your presentation, you've got to *look* at them. Remember, the audience is the *reason* you're speaking in the first place. Forget that and you've built a wall between you and your audience.

■THE RHYTHM OF EYE CONTACT

In my years as a speech coach, I've developed a unique technique that will help you learn quickly and efficiently how to involve your audience, keep them interested, and have them remember what you talked about. It's a technique that guarantees *total communication* between you and every member of your audience.

I call it the rhythm of eye contact. Simply put, your mouth should *never* be moving while your eyes are looking down. Your mouth should *never* be moving when you're looking away from your audience. You should *never* again:

Talk to your lectern
Talk to the floor
Talk to the back wall of the auditorium
Talk to the Lord or a fixture on the ceiling
Talk to your wristwatch
Talk to a visual aid or a prop

YOU LOSE when you talk to your slides, talk down to your notes, or talk up to the heavens. Mastering the Rhythm of Eye Contact will guarantee that you will always talk **to** your audience.

Again, for your listeners to consider themselves part of your talk, you have to be looking at them. This is how to do it:

To use the concept of the proper rhythm of eye contact, first consider the importance of the pause. No one can talk nonstop. We all have to pause. During the pause we glance down at our notes. Then we make the mistake of beginning to talk again, still looking down at our notes. The only eye contact we make is with our notes, not our audience.

Try this exercise, using the preceding paragraph as your manuscript text. Deliver each sentence, the words that follow in italics, to your mirror or to a friend. When you've finished each, pause and look down. Then say the next sentence looking *up* or to the friend or a mirror. Establish the rhythm for yourself.

No one can talk nonstop;

(Pause, look down. When you've seen what follows, look *up* and say:) *we all have to pause.*

(Pause, look down. When you've seen the next phrase, look up and say:) *During the pause we glance down at our notes.*

(Pause. Look down. Then look *up* and say:) *Then we make the mistake of beginning to talk again, still looking down at our notes.*

(Pause. Look down and then *up* again and say:) *The only eye contact we make is with our notes, not our audience.*

The pauses may seem artificial because the material is not your own. But even though they seem forced and endless, you're learning the rhythm of eye contact. Now try the exercise again, only this time open your face as you say each sentence to the friend or the image in the mirror. Again, practice the rhythm exactly as you did the last time but now add the element of the open face.

Now try the exercise one more time, adding a hand movement where you feel comfortable and where you think it's appropriate. And, above all, remember that you're not merely reading your notes or reciting sentences. You're communicating *ideas*. With an open face, an appropriate gesture, and words spoken *directly* to your audience, you'll get those ideas across.

This exercise is an ideal way to prepare and rehearse your delivery. If a sentence isn't easy to deliver with an open face and an occasional gesture, maybe it isn't a good sentence for you to say aloud. Maybe it's a signal that you aren't using the right words. And don't lose sight of the fact that the sentences that appear in this exercise are mine. If they don't come easily to you, change them. Make them your own. That's another cardinal rule. If someone else writes your material, don't begin to deliver it until you've made it your own. There is no speaking assignment so unimportant that it doesn't deserve complete preparation and concern for the audience. If you don't consider it important, don't agree to speak.

The best speakers are the best-prepared speakers. As you get more and more experience and begin to feel relaxed and comfortable, the preparation takes less time. President Reagan is a master of making printed text sound like spoken text. So, unless the situation is not a natural one for him, he doesn't require as much preparation to deliver a speech effectively as most other public officials do. But, interestingly, he has never learned the rhythm of eye contact technique. So, while he's expert at reading from the teleprompter, his one speaking weakness is demonstrated when he's forced to rely on a piece of paper in front of him. He still speaks to the paper too often.

Remember the vice presidential debate between George Bush and Geraldine Ferraro? She made the classic mistake of addressing her remarks to the lectern. It looked as though she were totally dependent on what was written on note cards or manuscript. She actually needed nothing. I'm not even certain she had any papers at all. She should have directed her remarks to her audience. Instead, she addressed her lectern.

In the debate format, she could have looked at the reporter

YOU WIN when you talk directly to your audience with an open face and appropriate gestures. **Be yourself** and you'll come across a winner every time.

who asked her the question. She could have looked into the camera, since the debate was being directed to those of us watching at home. She could have looked at people in the live studio audience. She could have looked at her opponent. I believe another look at the television coverage of the debate would show Ms. Ferraro addressing the lectern about 70 percent of the time. In fact, her most powerful moment was when she looked directly at Mr. Bush and told him she didn't need a lesson in foreign affairs.

Remember, you're here for your audience. Deliver to them. If you can master the rhythm of eye contact and combine it with an open face and an open body and a quiet, warm delivery, the audience will perceive you as caring for them, and they'll care back. You'll get your message across and everybody will be a winner.

THE "BABY" TECHNIQUE

One final word about your attitude or your approach to trying these techniques. Watch someone who's talking to a baby. Notice that he or she is:

Looking at the baby. There's no distraction in the eye contact.
Really exaggerating the concept of the open face with absolutely no self-consciousness.
Using gesture freely and without inhibition.
Talking quietly and with great animation, using extreme pitch change and rate variation, and is filled with enthusiasm, energy, and warmth.

When in doubt, as you prepare and rehearse your speech, pretend you're talking to a baby, and that will help you open up. And once you've mastered all of these skills and techniques, it won't matter whether you're accompanied to the lectern by a manuscript, an outline, notes, or nothing at all. You'll be able to deliver a dynamic talk instead of making an "ahem," pompous, dull speech.

■ COURTESY

I haven't mentioned it before, but speaking to a friend, fellow workers, or an audience is an act of *courtesy*. And it's just plain courteous to think of your audience before yourself. Courtesy is involved in preparing a speech. You prepare a speech because the audience *wants* it. It's courteous to be interesting instead of dull. You are interesting because it's what they *deserve*. Courtesy is a key ingredient in the concept of making intellectual love to your audience.

You shouldn't be improving your speaking skills just to look great in front of an audience—to be a star. Your goal must be to do better for the audience, to give them the best information in the best possible way. That's what separates the pleasing speaker from the bore.

Every time you open your mouth and words come out, they should be for the benefit of the listener. How many times have you seen political or show business personalities on television who appear to be making the appearance to glorify themselves instead of trying to edify the rest of us? They don't seem to care about us, only to promote their own egos, power, and careers. You and I don't matter to them. *They* matter to themselves. They're *discourteous*.

You and I are in danger of appearing that way if we don't adhere to the principles that the audience must come first— always. That's what courtesy is all about.

Communication is only effective when it's a giving, a sharing of ideas, getting the message to your audience in a way that is effortless for them, even if it is an effort for you.

You make this effort when you're talking to a baby. You want the baby to know you care. Why hold back just because you're talking to adults? You make this effort when you're telling your favorite joke. You do it when you tell secrets and gossip. Why not emulate the wonderful communication skills involved in these scenarios? Speaking as expressively as possible in every communication situation is true courtesy. It also happens to be good communication.

Think about what we call small talk—"Good morning," "Have a nice day," "What's up?" "How ya' doing?" "Lousy weather," "How are things?" We tend to simply utter the sounds. That's exactly what makes them small talk. We either don't care about a response, or we don't expect one. This is a mistake and it leads us into the worst habit of all—not caring, not communicating courteously.

It afflicts us on the telephone, on the elevator (if we speak at all), on the street, and in all our more formal communication situations. One man had these wonderful words for me after a workshop: "You've just saved my marriage." He realized that his wife and children had been seeing him at his worst. He'd looked disinterested and sounded tired and uncaring. He even realized that his wife frequently had asked him, "Why are you always so angry?" And he wasn't angry. His signals were wrong. He was making no effort. If it's worth saying, it's worth taking the time and trouble to say it as if you mean it and to look as if you mean what you're saying.

- The effective speaker is pleasant and interesting to see.
- The effective speaker is pleasant and interesting to listen to.
- The effective speaker delivers his message with all the meaning and feeling necessary for the audience to understand effortlessly.
- The effective speaker comes across to the audience as a sincere person with a genuine desire to get the material across.

Simplicity. Clarity. Brevity. Directness. Warmth. That's a brief composite of the components of courtesy.

▪ BEGINNING, ENDING—AND IN BETWEEN

Make sure you open your speech with a "grabber," a beginning designed to get immediate interest. Then make sure your ending is strong. A powerful ending will help you eliminate those awful two words so many speakers use, "Thank you." They're the speaker's equivalent of the Warner Brothers cartoon ending, "That's all, folks." It says, "I don't know how else to wrap this up." No one knows for sure, but I seriously doubt that Lincoln said, "that government of the people, by the people, for the people shall not perish from the earth. Thank you."

Finish strong, nod, and go. Or finish strong, nod, step back, then come forward to the microphone again and solicit questions, if that's what your host has asked you to do.

Watch your language. Eliminate obscenity, forgo ethnic slurs, don't do anything that may be offensive to someone in the audience. I learned this lesson the hard way. I had no idea that I was offending people with language I considered perfectly acceptable. But the fact that some people find even *hell* or *damn* truly offensive words tells me that you and I don't need to use those or stronger words. Again, anything that calls attention to itself or causes your audience embarrassment is bad technique. Anything that distracts your audience from what you've just said while you're still talking is bad technique.

If you're not noted for your joke-telling skill, don't try it in the formal speaking situation. It's deadly, and more often than not, the audience has heard the joke before. Only a great storyteller can make a joke funny on second or third hearing.

I worked with a man who wouldn't start a speech without telling three short jokes. I'm certain he once took a speech course and the only thing he remembered from it was "Be sure to break the ice with something funny." It was bad advice for him because he wasn't a very good storyteller. I tried in the gentlest way I could to make him aware that he was really turning his audience off with a series of "groaners," but to this day he's still opening every speech with three bad jokes.

When you prepare your text, make sure to use a lot of periods. Replace the commas, the dashes, the semicolons. When you deliver your text, speaking without pauses is the equivalent of writing without punctuation. A short sentence followed by a pause is an effective sentence. Period.

Get rid of acronyms, jargon, legalese, governmentese, words designed to impress, and words that make the audience stop and wonder as you proceed. As a final act of courtesy, when you think you've about perfected the text of your speech, before you begin to practice your delivery, make one last trip through the manuscript with a sharp pencil. Cut out a third. Very rarely is a speech too short. It's almost always too long.

If you take the time to know what you're going to say and say it . . . if you take the time to practice how you can say it best and say it that way . . . you can be a winner.

WHEN IT REALLY COUNTS

II

WINNING

THE

CONFRONTATION

I t's amazing how adversarial our contemporary American society has become. I think this is attributable in a large measure to the advent and popularity of "investigative reporting" on television. It seems that every question we hear a reporter ask is based on a negative assumption and contains an accusation and a loaded buzz-word or even a series of buzz-words. So a President is asked by a hard-nosed reporter *not* "What is your position on financial aid to the poor?" but rather "Why are you refusing to help the needy?" We hear a congressman eager to make the evening news asking the chemical company executive *not* "What action are you taking to clean up the toxic waste site?" but rather "Why are you poisoning our land, water, and air?"

Sound familiar? It should, it's what we're exposed to daily—people looking not for information, but hoping to expose a scandal. And sadly, we've all picked up the technique. Otherwise nice people, otherwise mild-mannered folks, otherwise gentle souls become monsters in the public forum. More and more we're becoming a society of inquisitors and crucifiers rather than debaters and discussers. It used to be that civilized people could talk about sensitive subjects—politics, religion, education, abortion. Now we've become a society of accusers, screamers, yellers, arguers. It becomes uncomfortable to be part of a confrontation whether as a participant or, worse, as an observer. When two people are shouting at each other, seemingly refusing to hear (or I should say listen to) the other point of view, we usually become embarrassed unless one of the screamers is representing a point of view very dear to us personally.

Some scenarios you may have witnessed or even been a participant in might include:

The school board announces a school closing in your neighborhood.

The city is planning to issue a permit for a drug rehabilitation center on your block.

A street near your home is being rezoned commercial for a supermarket with all the traffic pouring onto your street.

Your taxes are about to be doubled.

A chemical plant nearby is suspected of toxic discharges.

An abortion clinic plans to open on your street.

Teachers, police, firemen, garbage collectors, or nurses announce a strike.

Your brand-new car is a lemon.

The house you bought recently has major defects the realtor never bothered to tell you about.

The kid next door is playing what he laughingly calls music— deafeningly.

We've become so used to the reporter, the congressman, the neighbor using the offensive technique of the loaded question that we do it ourselves. Everyday situations become confrontations and we are intimidated by reporters, lawyers, public officials, our colleagues and coworkers, and even our neighbors. Intimidation has become a way of life. So we dread making a speech. We fear taking the witness stand. We're traumatized by the prospect of appearing on television. We fear that someone will try to tear us apart in public. We don't know how to handle confrontation. Will we get angry, get defensive, shout back, or fall apart?

Intimidation is a technique too many people have learned. It has replaced common courtesy. It's become fashionable to intimidate. Pushing other people around has become a talent or a skill almost universally practiced. We've learned the wrong lessons, and I place the blame squarely on the shoulders of aggressive TV journalists, whose salaries seem in direct proportion to their ability to make another human being look bad or at least to sweat a lot in public. Certainly there's a place for good, substantive investigative journalism, and tough questions can also be fair questions. The trick is learning how to handle them.

I started out in this area of communications training, helping business people become aware of the techniques used by reporters whose main goal was to *make* a story rather than report one. I focused on the communication skills that would help them beat these unethical reporters at their own game. Then I realized that the same techniques were applicable to all public demonstrations of arrogance, rudeness, intimidation, confrontation, and heckling. I've studied the methods used by the confronters and the techniques that can defeat them. You can learn to use those techniques to win an audience over to your side when someone is trying to make you look bad.

First of all, there are a few facts to realize about an audience, almost any audience. As I said earlier, there are only four ways people can judge you when they're seeing you for the first time—they can like you; they can dislike you; they can be neutral to you (uncaring about you), or they can feel sorry for you. Of course it's possible for them to feel sorry for and like or dislike you. But the point here is that your goal should be to communicate to the audience, not the harasser, and the best way to get your message across to your audience is to *be liked*.

Also, almost always, there are three points of view represented in an audience when the subject is volatile, controversial, and emotional. Some of the people in the audience already share your point of view—forget them. They're already on your side. Some of the people already have made up their minds on the other side of the issue, your adversary's side—forget them. You won't make converts in the short time you have. Remember that the object of your communication should always be the people whose minds are not yet made up. They haven't yet made a final judgment. That's how elections are won. That's how court cases are decided.

Take the abortion question, for example. People fervently debating that issue, whether brilliant or terrible, are not going to change each other's view on one of the most difficult subjects of the 1980s. The winner of that debate will be the person who most appeals to the undecided in the audience. The good debater can't possibly win over the people on the other side. The awful debater can't possibly lose the people who share his or her ideology. So your goal is to be liked by the people who haven't made up their minds. That's the objective and it establishes a brand-new set of ground rules in a confrontational situation. These new rules are:

- Pause. Think before you speak.
- Stay calm and reasonable.
- Don't get angry. Keep total control of your temper.
- Refuse to take any attack personally.
- Be positive.
- Give information rather than denials.
- Be explanatory. Don't succumb to the temptation to argue.
- Take lots of time. Let your opponent rush, shout, run off at the mouth, argue, yell, and scream. By taking your time, you'll infuriate him or her even further and make your opponent appear irrational to the audience you're trying to win.
- Be the voice of reason.
- Be the good guy, Mr. or Ms. Nice.
- Make intellectual love to your audience.

How do you do all this? I can hear you saying, "That's easy for you to say." Well, there are certain techniques that I've found really work. You've learned how important it is to please the audience with your face, your body, and your voice. But even if you're doing everything right, there may be some members of your audience you *cannot* please. Obviously, the hostile questions or the confrontational remarks are not going to come from your supporters. Those who have not yet made up their minds will usually remain silent. So you have to learn how to handle your adversaries. And here are the techniques you can use to do that.

■PAUSE (THINK BEFORE YOU SPEAK)

The most important technique is the *pause*. It's also the hardest to accomplish in taking control of what might otherwise be an uncontrollable situation.

We naturally react and *want* to react quickly—don't. It's unnatural to stop and think before we speak. In fact, it's so unnatural that we've developed a whole vocabulary of spoken pauses—audible pauses—pauses filled with strange, extraneous sounds. The most common, of course, is the sound "uh." And don't think for a second that it only afflicts the little guy who isn't used to confrontation. The mayor of New York City is a charming, witty, charismatic character named Edward Koch. But Mayor Koch can't seem to get out four consecutive words without the sound "uh" appearing. I know people who swear that they once heard him say, "I'm . . . uh . . . proud to . . . uh . . . be the . . . uh . . . mayor of New . . . uh . . . uh . . . York."

How about the TV newspersons? Without their teleprompters feeding them the words, they turn to mush just like the rest of us. I have a vivid recollection of Liberty Day, July 4, 1986. The networks were on the air for endless hours, and the reporters had no scripts much of the time. I remember Dan Rather saying something like "And now . . . uh . . . let's . . . uh . . . go to the . . . uh . . . New York harbor and . . . uh . . . our CBS chief correspondent . . . uh . . . Walter Cronkite. Walter, . . . uh . . . where are you . . . uh . . . now?"

Walter Cronkite, the dean of network news, replied, "Well, . . . uh . . . Dan, . . . just now we're . . . uh . . . passing . . . uh . . . the . . . uh . . . Statue of . . . uh . . . uh . . ." By then the listeners were ready to shout, *"Liberty, Walter, Liberty!"*

On July 31, 1987, Secretary of Defense Caspar Weinberger, testifying before a congressional committee, offered no illuminating explanation in reply to a question about the importance of continuing aid to the Contras: "I think it's even more vital now that . . . uh . . . all of this . . . uh . . . uh . . . all of these . . . uh . . . uh . . . attempts or whatever it were that were made . . . uh . . . to . . . uh . . . assist in . . . uh . . . uh . . . uh . . . non- . . . uh . . . uh . . . mmmuh . . . straightforward and . . . uh . . . and . . . uh . . . means that are provided for in our regular statutory . . . uh . . . uh . . . framework—that none of that distract us from the basic importance and and essential correctness of the . . . uh . . . of the requirement of . . . of . . . supporting the . . . uh . . . the . . . uh . . . democratic resistance in Nicaragua."

The athlete has popularized the expression *Ya know.* Most of us overuse *I think.* And two other meaningless pauses in our vocabularies are *And so* and *like.* You've heard President Reagan's "Well" before every answer at a news conference. And how about *uh, er, mmm,* and all the other noises we make when we're pausing aloud? Sometimes we use whole sentences: "I'm glad you asked me that question," and the memorable "Let me make one thing perfectly clear." These are spoken attempts to get the mind in gear. Instead, *stop and think.* It's difficult. It's even unnatural. But it's an essential first step.

A classic three-word print ad has run many times that says exactly what I'm telling you to try to do. It reads:

ready

FIRE

aim

That says it all. We're too quick to fire off the mouth before taking aim with the mind. And unless we put our minds in gear before we move our mouths, we may not be able to reach our audiences with the best, most pertinent information we have available to us.

The, "ah," person who makes, "uh," sounds while, "er," talking seems unsure, uncertain of where he or she is going, insecure, and unused to thinking on his feet. The silent pause helps your audience create a more positive image of you. It also throws your adversary off balance. Did you hear the question? How are you going to reply to the hostile remark? And while your adversary is wondering, you're thinking, framing your reply. You are in control of the situation, not your adversary.

EYE CONTACT (LOOK AT YOUR ADVERSARY)

The second thing to do as you pause is to maintain eye contact with the person who's being aggressive, confrontational, intimidating, obnoxious. That doesn't mean staring directly into this person's eyes. It means finding a comfortable place on his or her face and keeping your eyes there. Don't let your eyes wander. Like the audible pause, the pause filled with sound, eye movement tends to make an audience think "dishonest," "shifty-eyed," "untrustworthy," "looking for a way out of a bad situation." But if you look directly at your adversary, you will give the impression of being honest, thoughtful, reasonable, and trustworthy. And once again, your adversary is thrown off balance, wondering what's coming next. *He* won't know where to look. *You* are in control.

BE POSITIVE IN YOUR REPLY

A pause will give you valuable time to frame your answer to a hostile or loaded question. As you do so, first eliminate the negative—the accusations and the buzz-words—from the questions. By all means, answer the question and answer honestly. That's most important. But don't give the questioner what he or she is looking for—don't repeat his buzz-words. Don't deny his accusations. Don't tell him he's wrong or that he has his facts mixed up. Even though we do these things quite naturally, believe it or not, they're wrong. They're wrong from the perspective of winning the audience. Use the pause to figure out what the real question is and how you are going to answer it. If you take an attack personally or try to deny or to negate a hostile question, you'll play right into your adversary's hands.

▪ GIVE VALUABLE INFORMATION

After eliminating the negative, the accusations, and the buzz-words, use the pause to give your mind time to shape an honest, complete, positive answer to the question, an answer you can give with *pride*. It's amazing how this single concept can change the whole course of a confrontation. It can make you a winner because now you're sharing valuable information rather than using valuable time to reinforce negatives. You're telling your audience what you want it to remember rather than denying what your adversary wants it to remember.

Some examples will help clarify this simple but effective technique for winning any confrontation. Remember, the technique is to replace the negative, the accusations, and the buzz-words with facts, positive information, and pride.

In the format of a television interview, I asked a chemical company employee in a training session a question I mentioned earlier, "Why are you poisoning our air?" Before learning the technique for handling such questions, he answered negatively and defensively, as perhaps 95 percent of other people in the same spot would answer. He said, "We're *not* poisoning the air." Before he could go on, I pulled the microphone back to me and asked a second hostile question. He gave me a second denial. By playing according to the wrong rules, he gave two incorrect answers to two equally nasty, accusatory, negative questions. He didn't seize the opportunity to make his point. So he reinforced mine. Simply put, I was in control. As the training proceeded, we tried it again. "Why are you poisoning our air?" I demanded angrily. He paused, looked at me directly, and replied, "Our company has spent $18 million to bring our emissions standards to a point that exceeds federal, state, and local requirements."

Another example. I asked a trucking company chairman, "Why do you allow your drivers to kill and maim?" You can guess his answer, right? He said without even a moment for breath, "Our drivers don't kill and maim." And because he took the attack personally, he had a snarl on his face when he said it. Later, he said in reply to the same hostile question, "Last year our safety rate was the *best* in the entire industry. We had millions of highway miles without a fatality. It's an exceptional record and I'm really proud of it." What a difference.

When you repeat the negative, the accusations, and the buzz-words, the audience remembers the accuser's words. When you answer with information, facts, and positive, proud statements, the audience remembers your answers. You take full control.

If you have nothing to be ashamed of and nothing to hide, you have no reason to fear a confrontation. It's quite remarkable how well a well-trained person does in a public confrontation. The more unreasonable the confronter gets, the greater your opportunity to win. And remember, if no one wins, *you lose.*

The pause is really the key. If you pause, you can allow your mind to concentrate on these ground rules for handling confrontation. If you give an instant response, it will invariably be a negative—a denial, a defense. The pause also allows you to be in control of the rhythm of the confrontation. An aggressor can't stand it if you prove yourself a thinker, a reasonable person. The aggressor expects you to get emotional. The aggressor expects you to get angry. The aggressor expects you to become irrational. But the aggressor doesn't know what to do if you stay calm and reasonable. You actually make him furious with you.

Try this sometime. An angry driver doesn't like something you just did or didn't do. He's furious with you. He opens his window, shouts obscenities, gives you the finger, and looks for all the world as if he'd like to run you off the road. Smile. Wave hello. Mouth the words "Good morning" with an open face. He'll be flabbergasted. He won't recover. He might become even more furious. But maybe—just maybe—he'll shake his head and smile back.

The technique works. It works in business situations, in personal situations, and in the courtroom or the classroom. It works in negotiations, in sales. You name the place, it works. Try it. You'll like it.

⸀THE RADIO OR TELEVISION INTERVIEW

In a TV interview, you're not on your home field. Even if the actual interview is done in your office or your home, the cameras, lights, microphones, miles of cables, crews of technicians, makeup people, and others, all make the situation strange, frightening, intimidating. Anyone who agrees to appear on a show like "60 Minutes" without training *specifically* for that appearance is inviting a disaster. In fact, television is such a powerful medium that it's worth training to make a better impression on a local show or a video that will be seen only by colleagues and coworkers.

Television offers the greatest opportunity a communicator has today. If you spent the rest of your life on the phone or making speeches to community groups, you'd never be able to reach as many people as you'll reach in a single TV interview. TV interviews dominate our impressions of entire industries. Mass judgments are made based on the appearance of a single representative. TV can make or break a political candidate. So be prepared. It's your big chance to sell yourself, your ideas, your organization, and your entire profession.

United Press International released the results of a poll concerning TV and film stardom. The result was that the main element is likability. It's hard to concentrate on being likable or on the impression you're making on an audience when your sweat glands and your heart rate are running wild. But it's the *audience* that counts. You *can* look good, you *can* make a positive impression, you *can* get your message across more effectively if you follow the winning techniques talked about in the earlier chapters. And if you find yourself in a confrontational situation, you *can* beat your adversary and be liked by the undecided members of the audience.

Even the worst question gives you the opportunity to make a favorable impression if you pause, then give an honest, positive, complete answer from a perspective of pride. The advantage that a TV reporter or interviewer has is that you're playing his game and you're playing on his court. Your advantage is that you have the information. If you learn the rules of the game, you can win consistently. Pay particular attention the next time you see a newspaper "correction" item. Notice that the first words are an acknowledgment that the paper made a mistake in a story or an editorial comment. Then it tells you what it *should have said*. It almost never tells you exactly what it said originally. It never *repeats* its original error. It learned to play the game long ago. In fact, it established the ground rules. So, if the journalistic community refuses to repeat its own mistake, why should you repeat a mistaken accusation about you? Give the facts as they are, as the reporter should have known them, and as you want your audience to understand them.

Time is a vital factor in television. The evening news program is thirty minutes long. Of that, maybe twenty-two minutes is news, the rest is commercials, promos for later programs on this station, introductions, and credits. Then subtract more minutes for sports, weather, and happy talk. So all you have is a small part of, say, a minute-and-twenty-second segment. Your actual participation will consist of two or three "sound bites." A sound bite is you on camera speaking. You'll be on for around seven seconds, then another twelve seconds, and if it's a really hot story, another fifteen seconds. That's your time on the evening news. The rest of your story involves the anchor person setting up the story, the reporter asking you the two or three questions, then the reporter winding up the story and identifying himself and his location.

In the time allotted to you, your job is to get out information.

There's no time for denials like "We don't kill and maim" or "We don't rape the land." There's no time for angry responses like "You don't know what you're talking about" or "You don't have the correct information." Instead, tell the reporter what you know that you feel the audience should know. Some unforgettable examples come to mind.

In New York City a man took organized groups of people on what he called "Eating Tours" of Central Park. He charged a small amount of money, and on the walk he pointed out what grew that was edible and would snip off samples. His clients would then taste the edibles. One day he was given a summons for defacing the park, and when the press got hold of the story, they thought they had the makings of a good bureaucratic scandal. The parks commissioner was asked why he had agreed to issue a summons to a decent citizen who was just making an imaginative living and harming no one while drug dealers and other unsavory characters were also operating in the park. He answered in two short, snappy, simple, understandable sentences. He said, "He's not eating *in* the park. He's *eating the park.*" Case closed.

A man being interviewed on TV was stunned to be asked the question "Doesn't it bother you to work for a company that makes obscene profits?" After a short pause, the man smiled and said, "I guess you didn't know that your network made more money last year than my company." (He named the network and his company.)

Many women and men with high profiles in their companies and their communities attend training sessions for that very reason. They are often the targets of the media. A police chief in a California beach community told me, "Two days after your session, a bike path in our town was the scene of some random gunshots. We cordoned off the area and had a helicopter overhead. Fortunately, there were no injuries, but a reporter grabbed me and yelled over the sound of the chopper, 'A resident tells me this bike path has attracted all the riffraff, all the undesirables from Long Beach and that there's constant danger to the folks who live nearby. That's true, isn't it?' I was about to say, 'No, it isn't. It's *not dangerous*. We're *not* attracting trash.' But I caught myself. I paused. I remembered your training and was able to give the real facts. I said, 'The residents of this town fought hard for this bike path. They use it. They love it, and they're very proud of it.'" The story that appeared was very favorable and reflected well on the police and the entire community.

A developer in the Southwest said, "Right after your training, I was swamped by reporters. The questions were rapid-fire and awful. 'Why are you raping our city?' 'Why are you willing to create a traffic nightmare here?' 'Who gave you the right to play God here?' And more. I was mad as hell, but I paused, collected my thoughts, and gave them positive answers. One by one, I explained why this project would be good for the city, how it would benefit the residents and visitors, what the actual traffic studies showed, and how a very hostile city council had turned around and supported the project when they learned the facts."

If you need extra time to think, there are some wonderful phrases that will lead you down the right path:

I'm proud to be able to tell you . . .
Let me explain what the facts really are . . .
I'd like to clear up a misunderstanding. What we really do is . . .
That's a strange question. Let me think about that for just a second . . .

Of course if you're not the right person to answer the question, say so and offer to put the reporter in touch with the right person, or offer to get the information and get back to him. And never be afraid to say (if it's honest), "I don't understand the question." The two worst things you can do are answer a question when you don't know the answer and answer when you don't know what the questioner is asking.

A corollary: Never avoid the reporter. Never say "No comment." Never appear to be uncooperative. My rule is this. Unless you've just embezzled $800,000 from your employer, you have no reason to avoid talking to the media. If you can be honest, you can win. Audiences love honesty. They appreciate the truth, especially when it's told with style, confidence, and skill.

A word about your relationship with the media and your attitude toward them is in order here. Whether we like it or not, whether we admit it or not, we're all filled with personal and political biases. The media is no exception. Some reporters have come to mistrust elected officials and business people. Their background and training demand impartiality, so they won't even admit a bias to themselves. They can quote chapter and verse about cases involving corrupt politicians and greedy business people and not realize that they've mistakenly concluded that every politician is on the take and every business person is without integrity or conscience. Of course, it's a false assumption.

Many elected officials and people in business have a similar mistrust of the press. I've heard dozens of each say, "I never get quoted right," "The story is always slanted against me no matter what I say," or worse, "I hate reporters. They're just looking to make mincemeat out of you." Many absolutely refuse to talk to a reporter.

Each side may have very good reason to mistrust the other, but together they've built up a crisis of confidence. Good reporters, and there are a lot of them, want facts not scandal. Sure, if there's scandal material, that's fine. But if there isn't, that's fine, too. Yet, there are also those reporters and interviewers who try to create scandal even if none exists. The difference is in the "slant" of their questions—"Why did the board decide to take this action?" versus "Why does your board rip off the stockholders?"

About ten years ago, when I was working closely with the United States Chamber of Commerce, a colleague called members of Washington's business press to announce a news conference on an issue the Chamber considered to be one of the major ones in the upcoming session of Congress. One of the most prominent business reporters in the country declined the invitation, saying something like "You guys are the spokesmen for business. I wouldn't trust what you say for a minute."

The business community has brought that response on itself. For decades the good public relations officer was the one who could get the chairman out the back door when the press was on the front steps. With a few notable exceptions, business never realized that the media represented the best possible way to reach the public.

Politicians have no alternative. The media is the single most important factor in every major political campaign. And the candidate who ignores that fact, who lacks the skills necessary to use the media to reach the voters, who lacks the techniques necessary to debate an opponent or handle a hostile reporter does so at his or her own peril. The day after he was defeated in the presidential election of 1980, Walter Mondale still found time and energy to wrap up his campaign with the press people who had followed him through it. There was nothing on the line for him anymore. He opened his face and said, more warmly than I've ever heard him say anything, "I guess I just never learned how to get my message across to you."

If you can handle a confrontation, you can handle any speaking situation. A final word of caution—don't allow yourself to be "suckered." There are attorneys, reporters, and other professionals who are trained in the skills of catching you with your guard down. They'll ask you a short series of very easy questions to get you in the rhythm of answering quickly, "off the top of your head." Then, with their rhythm established, they'll throw the zinger at you. Now, you're most likely to blurt out the first thing that springs into your mind. So, once again, establish *your* rhythm. Pause and look at your adversary *before* you answer a question in front of an audience, a camera, or a jury. This is your mind's strongest defense against your making an ass of yourself in public. And, during the pause, use your mind to do what one student of mine said he learned to do: "Reword the question the way you wish it had been asked." Then answer *that* question with honesty, completeness, and pride.

▪ A CASE STUDY

No event created more interest than President Reagan's November 19, 1986, news conference. And no event can illustrate more clearly the necessity of learning, and using, the techniques necessary to handle a confrontation and get your message across.

What follows is a group of questions (not necessarily in exact sequence) the President was asked during that news conference, his answers, then my comments on the President's answers and my suggestions as to how he might have answered the questions better. I am not trying to second-guess the President. I'm basing my suggestions on the information he gave in his opening statement and on other things he said up to the time of the news conference.

QUESTION: Mr. President, in the recent past there was an administration whose byword was, watch what we do, not what we say. How would you assess the credibility of your own Administration in the light of the prolonged deception of Congress and the public in terms of your secret dealings with Iran, the disinformation, the trading of Zakharov for Daniloff? And I'd like to follow up.

THE PRESIDENT: Well, Helen, let me take the last one first. I know you, some, persist in saying that we traded Zakharov for Daniloff. We did not. We said that we would have no dealings with the Soviet Union even on going to Iceland until Daniloff was in our hands. But to bring it up to date on this, there was no deception intended by us. There was the knowledge that we were embarking on something that could be of great risk to the people we were talking to, great risk to our hostages, and therefore we had to have it limited to only the barest number of people that had to know. I was not breaking any law in doing that. It is provided for me to do that. At the same time I have the right under the law to defer reporting to Congress, to the proper congressional committees, on an action and defer it until such time as I believe it can safely be done with no risk to others. And that's why I have ordered in this coming week the proper committees will be debriefed on this and we—there are still some parts of this that we cannot go public with because it will bring to risk, endanger people that are held in, people that we had been negotiating with. We were not negotiating government to government. We were negotiating with certain individuals within that country.

This was obviously a very "loaded" question, accusing the President of deceiving both the Congress and the public. Rather then denying those accusations at length or rationalizing them, the President might have replied: Our dealings with both the Soviets and Iran demanded the utmost secrecy. The safety of the Americans still in captivity depended on tight security.

QUESTION: Mr. President, has Secretary Shultz discussed his resignation with you? Have you agreed to accept it, or have you asked him to stay on?

THE PRESIDENT: Mike, he has never suggested to me in our meetings that a resignation—and in fact he has made it plain that he will stay as long as I want him, and I want him. So, there's never been any discussion there. He knows that I want him to stay and he has, in advance, said that he wants to. There's been no talk of resignation.

The reporter has assumed that Shultz has offered his resignation, which may or may not have been true. Rather than denying that assumption, my suggested response: Secretary Shultz is a valued member of my team.

QUESTION: Mr. President, you have stated flatly, and you stated flatly again tonight, that you did not trade weapons for hostages. And yet the record shows that every time an American hostage was released—last September, this July, and again just this very month—there had been a major shipment of arms just before it. Are we all to believe that was just a coincidence?

THE PRESIDENT: Chris, the only thing I know about major shipments of arms is, as I've said, everything that we sold them could be put in one cargo plane and there would be plenty of room left over. Now, if there were major shipments—and we know this has been going on; there have been other countries that have been dealing in arms with Iran; there have been also private merchants of such things that have been doing the same thing.

Now, I've seen the stories about a Danish tramp steamer and Danish sailors' union officials talking about their ships taking various supplies to Iran. I didn't know anything about that till I saw the press on it, because we certainly never had any contact with anything of the kind.

And, so, this—it's just that we did something for a particular mission; there was a risk entailed. And Iran held no hostages; Iran did not kidnap anyone, to our knowledge, and the fact that part of the operation was that we knew, however, that the kidnappers of our hostages did have some kind of relationship in which Iran could at times influence them—not always, but could influence them. And so three of our hostages came home.

Again, this is a very loaded question, which accuses the President of being a liar. My suggested response: The arms shipments never were intended to go to the people holding the hostages, and they didn't go to them.

QUESTION: If I may follow up, sir? On that first point, your own

Chief of Staff, Mr. Regan, has said that the U.S. condoned Israeli shipments of arms to Iran, and aren't you, in effect, sending the very same message you always said you didn't want to send? Aren't you saying to terrorists, either you or your state sponsor, which in this case was Iran, can gain from the holding of hostages?

THE PRESIDENT: No, because I don't see where the kidnappers or the hostage holders gained anything. They didn't get anything. They let the hostages go. Now whatever is the pressure that brought that about, I'm just grateful to it for the fact that we got them. As a matter of fact, if there had not been so much publicity, we would have had two more than we were expecting.

My suggested response: I can only repeat what I told you in my opening statement. We had four objectives in mind when we created this initiative. We wanted to help bring Iran back into the family of nations. We wanted to help end a devastating war. We wanted to help bring an end to terrorism. And we wanted to bring our people held in captivity home. That was our message.

QUESTION: Sir, if I may, the polls show that a lot of American people just simply don't believe you. That the one thing that you've had going for you more than anything else in your presidency—your credibility—has been severely damaged. Can you repair it? What does it mean for the rest of your presidency?

THE PRESIDENT: Well I imagine I'm the only one around who wants to repair it and I didn't have anything to do with damaging it.

My suggested response: I made the decision knowing full well that if we succeeded there were rewards, and that if it failed, there were potential damages. I think the American people will agree that getting our hostages home and our other three goals were well worth some risks.

From this abbreviated exchange I call your attention to a few facts I hope are obvious. The President could have benefited greatly from the pause. He could have used the pause to figure out what the question was or how convoluted it really was. Or he could have asked the reporter to rephrase the question to clarify its meaning.

He could have shaped his answers by removing the buzz-words and the negatives. Too often he repeated and reinforced negatives and said what his policy wasn't rather than what it was.

He went on too long. Like so many of us, he seemed to have an aversion to stopping when he had finished. And that's exactly when the foot enters the mouth.

Finally, he shouldn't have been afraid (and you shouldn't be afraid) to say "I don't know" or "I don't understand your question." Most people, and I include the President, are truly reluctant to admit that they don't know everything.

Of course the President occupies a unique position in our public life. But all of us, whatever our jobs, will inevitably come up against confrontation in some form in our personal and professional lives. It may come from a coworker or colleague, an angry neighbor, a reporter, or a heckler. You can win that confrontation if you pause, take aim, and get ready with a positive answer *before* you fire.

WINNING

TESTIMONY

There was a time when our knowledge of legal procedures and the courtroom was limited to TV programs ("Perry Mason") or films (*Witness for the Prosecution*). Now, with so many people suing or investigating each other and with most of us embracing and speaking out for causes, we may find ourselves involved in a court case or a legislative proceeding. And to testify effectively requires considerable skill.

Like a television or a radio interview, delivering testimony takes place on "foreign soil." We're asked to appear in strange surroundings and that can adversely affect our ability to play the game. Also, like the radio or TV interview, giving testimony is often a confrontational situation. You may have a patient and friendly questioner who guides you through your testimony, or you may have an impatient and hostile questioner who is trying to prove you are lying through your teeth. What are you supposed to say? How are you supposed to react? In court and in hearings, every appearance is different but the communication skills are similar.

THE DEPOSITION

Before a trial begins, more often than not depositions are taken. A deposition is simply a pretrial statement made under oath before attorneys for both sides and a clerk. There is no jury and usually no judge. Supposedly the deposition helps prepare the two sides for the courtroom and shortens the trial time. The key words here are *under oath*. If you fail to tell the truth in a deposition, it's as bad as if you lied in the actual courtroom.

The entire difference between the deposition and courtroom testimony is that in the deposition only substance counts. There is no judgmental audience except for the attorneys, and they can't acquit or convict. They can't bring the case to its conclusion. So only the mind is involved. Face, body, and voice hardly come into play in the deposition. It is a confrontational situation, however, so the pause is once again your most effective weapon. When you are asked a question, think *before* you speak. Pause, take aim, get ready, fire. And, needless to say, your answer should be the truth.

It probably seems like an oversimplification, but honesty and the pause are the only tools you'll need in the deposition. The pause gives you the opportunity to consider the question, its meaning and its consequences, before you answer. And honesty means you won't perjure yourself. If you tell the truth, you never have to remember what you said.

If you don't know, *say so.* If you don't understand the question, *say so.*

And the pause in every scenario allows your attorney to interject with a point or an objection.

▪THE COURTROOM TRIAL

With the presence of a judge and possibly a jury to determine the outcome of a case, the skills of face, body, and voice become vitally important in giving testimony. Yes, the ground rules for the deposition also apply here, but how the jury *perceives* you is critical. Don't forget that the jury is an audience and it can like you, dislike you, feel sorry for you, or be neutral to you. Your job, along with being truthful, is to be liked, because the jury will then believe you're telling the truth. No one will ever know how many people guilty of heinous crimes have been set free because the jury liked them. Conversely, I'll bet a lot of innocent people have been convicted because the jury thought they looked like criminals. But most juries, like most audiences, are not easily deceived. They believe what they hear if what they see makes it believable.

The open face, the genuine and appropriate gesture, and the warm, friendly voice are the weapons most likely to help you win a jury to your side. If you need a villain, let it be the opposing attorney. Remember how effective Lieutenant Colonel Oliver North was during his testimony before a joint congressional committee in the Iran/Contra hearings? He kept his own emotions under control. He gave evidence of being upset by certain questions, but he never lost his cool. He left the outbursts to his attorney. Whether or not he was telling the truth, he gained the respect of the committee and the American public.

When you're on the stand, take a short pause before answering even the simplest question, and answer in a full sentence.

"What is your name?"

(Pause) "My name is . . ."

"What is your address?"

(Pause) "I live at . . ."

"How long have you lived there?"

(Pause) "I've been there since . . ."

Now the adversarial attorney has been put on notice. This witness will not be intimidated. This witness will not be tricked into blurting out answers. This witness knows what he's doing.

Appearing as a witness in a trial is obviously a stressful situation. So before you testify use proper breathing techniques for relaxation and control. If you look nervous and apprehensive, it might easily be mistaken for dishonesty. Think about people you've seen moistening their lips and shifting their eyes back and forth. They look intimidated and often seem to be groping for a way out or a dishonest answer. Three rules to follow during your testimony—answer *only* the question that has been asked, don't elaborate, don't volunteer information. Always be brief and to the point. It is, after all, the opposing attorney's job to discredit your testimony. It is your job to convince the jury that you're telling the truth. As in any confrontation, you can turn negative questions into positive answers. And the communication skills of mind, body, and voice will do the rest in convincing the jury to decide in your favor.

CONGRESSIONAL TESTIMONY

An appearance before a committee of the U.S. Senate or House of Representatives is unlike any other experience. We've seen many examples of this on television. Some have been good, most have been terrible. The most familiar image is that of the witness who opens his attaché case, takes out an eighty-page manuscript, hunches over the text, and says to the page, "Mr. Chairman, members of this distinguished committee, my name is . . ." And on he drones until the last word is read in a dull monotone and everybody has fallen asleep.

There's no excuse for that kind of testimony. Very few people, including professional lobbyists, realize there's a regulation on the books that says that testimony before Congress will be a summary of what's been previously submitted. The person who reads the entire submission in a dull monotone is just plain being rude to Congress and is in violation of the rules.

If you are called upon to testify before Congress, first, submit the full text of your statement, as required, forty-eight or seventy-two hours before your appearance. Second, prepare a *very brief* summary of that statement for oral delivery. Put it in short, snappy sentences, to be spoken rather than read. Then begin your testimony, after the protocol, with "You have my full statement in front of you. Let me briefly summarize the highlights of that paper." Your listeners might even be induced to pay attention after that, knowing you plan to be mercifully brief and courteous.

Here is a brief rundown on some of the things I think your testimony should be:

Honest
Positive
Brief
Simple
Logical
Well-organized
Well-delivered
Anecdotal rather than statistical
A concise statement of your position

And, of course, in your delivery, all of the communication

skills are a necessity—the open face, appropriate gestures, voice control, directness, and courtesy. When you consider how much of Congress's time is spent in hearings, you'll realize how practical these guidelines are and how much better your chances of really getting your message across will become.

THE LOCAL HEARING

A hearing on a local issue is the scenario most of us are likely to encounter. It's the least intimidating arena and certainly the most familiar. It's also the one that we are more willing to become involved with. After all, a local issue is one that affects us directly and personally.

But, here again, I know people who are so intimidated by the public-speaking situation that they've refused to be active participants in local issues. They won't speak out in public meetings because they have that terrible debilitating fear—the fear of making a fool of themselves in public. It's an unreasonable fear, but that knowledge doesn't change anything.

Using good communication skills will make public speaking easier. Once more, I urge you to start off with proper breathing. It's the first step in the process of throwing off stress and gaining control of yourself. Be prepared. That alone will increase your self-confidence enormously. Then concentrate on making the briefest possible statement of your position. Five words usually have far more impact than five thousand. Be open. Be honest, direct, and courteous. Be personal. Tell the assembled group what this action will mean to them, their community, their pocketbooks, their neighborhoods—this kind of information has impact.

A local hearing is usually much less formal than a legislative hearing. Use the lack of formality to your advantage. Observe any protocol, but be as informal as you feel will help your cause. And talk quietly. Even if the issue is highly charged and the hearing is adversarial, don't get angry. Don't lose your temper. Above all, remember the rules of the confrontation. Turn negative questions into positive answers. If you pause and think before you speak, your words will have even greater impact.

If you've been consumed by fear and refused to participate in local issues, remember that your viewpoint is just as important as anyone else's. By practicing the skills and techniques of good communication that apply in any speaking situation, you will be able to make a difference in your community by getting your message across.

WINNING
THE JOB
INTERVIEW

One of the most stressful speaking situations is the job interview. And, unless I miss my guess, we've all been through it one time or another. If you really need that job, if it seems your whole life depends on it, the stress can be almost unbearable.

I have a friend who had worked hard all his life, earned a decent salary, reached a prestigious position in his field. Then suddenly, because of a merger, he found himself out of work, jobless. Because he and his wife had put several children through college and had supported more than one indigent family member, they had very few assets. And now, he had no job. After months of looking, his résumé made an impression on a potential employer and he was asked to come in for an interview.

My advice to my friend (and to you): "Whatever you do, don't panic." But "everything, everything, *everything* is riding on this one interview," you say. Maybe so, but if you're desperate and it shows, you haven't got a chance. That piece of advice is really the key to success in the job interview and in every other form of communication. When an interviewer or an audience sees you squirm, becomes aware of your desperation, you're almost certain to be a loser.

I've painted a grim scenario, but my advice is equally true for the college student looking for a post-graduation first full-time job. It's true for the woman who's been out of the job market raising a family, who's decided that her sanity and her financial situation require her to get back into the money-earning world. It's true for the man or woman who wants to change companies or jobs. And what is really important? The way you communicate; the way you're perceived by the person conducting the interview.

▪ WRONG IMPRESSIONS

The psychology involved in the typical job interview is false and destructive. It discourages honest communication. The interviewee tends to look on the interviewer as someone in a position of ultimate power. And this feeling grows in direct proportion to the real need for employment. "He controls my future. My fate is in his hands. He holds the key to restoring me to the ranks of respectability. He is the supreme judge of my worth and value. And he has a secure job in a position of influence and power. It's not fair." Not only is all of this true, but the interviewee suspects that his own unemployed status or job search will be perceived by the interviewer as a flaw or a weakness. After all, being unemployed or looking for another job (we think) is shameful, blameful, and a vulnerable condition. It's a classic guilt trip.

These dynamics can be horrifying. "How on earth can I ever explain how smart and skilled and knowledgeable I am in a few minutes to a perfect stranger?" To make it worse, quite often the interviewer's manner, style, and approach all reinforce these dynamics. So the stress for the interviewee is intensified, approaching the unbearable. In fact, the applicant who feels this desperation (and worse, shows it) will unwittingly magnify all these fears into a huge and haunting specter. Desperation always manages to show itself in the eyes. Insecurity is betrayed by the entire body. The face and hands send all the signals you hope to avoid. The voice quivers and trembles. And a mind in panic is in no condition to cope with the interview at hand.

WHAT CAN YOU DO?

First, as in any stressful situation, gain control of yourself by doing the breathing and relaxation exercises in Chapter 6.

Second, bring into play all of the basic communication skills you learned in Part I. Use your face, your voice, and your body to gain control over the situation rather than let it gain control over you.

Next, consciously adopt a counterpsychology. What allows you to do this is the knowledge that the intimidating dynamics of the job interview are false. They are negative. They have no reality. They are imaginings born of fear, stress, intimidation. Here are three factors to consider:

- Your worth and your value are in you. They have nothing to do with the fact of being employed, holding a job, earning money. You're the same person regardless of your situation.
- Your interviewer isn't intrinsically superior to you. Because of the transient circumstances of the moment, he or she is more powerful than you are. But the interviewer's power isn't ultimate. There are other jobs, other employers out there. You're a free person. You and your interviewer are essentially equal in two respects. You're both human beings and each may have something the other needs and wants. Only your roles are different. They could well be reversed. The interviewer needs to fill the job vacancy as much as the interviewee needs the job. And don't lose sight of the fact that you are also interviewing your interviewer about the job and about the company.
- You aren't just looking for *any* job—if you are, you could be making a world-class mistake—you're looking for the *right* job. You're looking for the job that will let you put your skills and experience to work most fully and productively, matching them to the needs of the employer. The purpose of the job interview, and never lose sight of this fact, is to determine whether those conditions prevail in *this* job.

Once you have put the job interview in its proper perspective, you gain new confidence. You're not cocky, insolent, or impolitic but confident. You understand the dynamics of the interview. You've learned how to play a new game, and you can play to win.

Confidence is the key word. Externally, it will allow you to be friendly, open, interested, straightforward, and. a good listener. Inside, you're alert, energized, and, on the deepest level, detached and objective. You're able to believe from the outset "If this works out, that will be fine. If it doesn't work out, that will be OK, too. This one may not be the perfect one." Confidence helps on every level. You come across as confident and poised. You're calm enough to think clearly and rationally. Your modest self-assurance is pleasant and attractive compared to the insecurity, nervousness, or overeagerness of other candidates. You really shouldn't want the job unless it's right for you or if the employer doesn't have the right enthusiasm for adding you to the team.

A friend of mine who's been a professional job counselor and whose help on the material for this chapter has been invaluable offers the following tip. If you're desperate for work, desperate for an income—any income—then take whatever job you can get that will bring in some money while the job search goes on. Work as a salesclerk in the evening. Take an early-morning delivery job. Work on a clean-up crew at night. Whatever you do need never show up on your résumé. There is no such thing as a demeaning job, only people who consider themselves too good to do certain kinds of work. Overqualified, yes. Demeaning, no.

▪Interview strategies

Once you have the right attitude about a job interview, there are certain strategies you can use both on your résumé and during the interview itself that will go a long way toward guaranteeing your success.

Identify Your Three or Four Strongest Skills or Areas of Experience

Most of us are not totally one dimensional. Unless we're just starting out in a career search or have had highly specialized technical careers, we probably have several strong suits. It's not unusual for someone to be skilled and have a background in more than one area: planning, organization management, production management, personnel management, budget and financial planning, systems design, sales, marketing, training and development, editing, public relations, communications . . . whatever. Analyze your work history to pinpoint precisely the central, basic categories of your skills and experience rather than the specific duties of a job you've held. For example, you were an analyst/administrator at the XYZ Corporation rather than program officer in charge of impact statements for the office of Environmental Compliance. The approach of highlighting your general skills has two main advantages. First, it's flexible, and *you're* flexible, depending on the needs of the potential employer. Second, it stands alone, stripped of ties to your previous employer and open to future applications. As your interviewer, I'm not so much interested in what your duties and responsibilities were in your last job as I am in what you can do for me.

CITE SPECIFIC EXAMPLES OF YOUR ACCOMPLISHMENTS IN MEASURABLE TERMS

Give numbers that quantify what you were responsible for, how effective you were, the changes you brought about, the volume you handled, the numbers of people you supervised, the increase in sales or productivity, the size of your budget, the scope of your function. Use whatever yardstick is appropriate— degrees of growth, improvement, or accuracy; honors and citations; promotions and bonuses; decrease in complaints; increase in income; membership, output, or stock value. These kinds of objective measurements say more about your ability and actual accomplishments than any claims you may make.

LEARN WHAT YOU CAN ABOUT YOUR POTENTIAL EMPLOYER AND THE BUSINESS

Learn what you can about the company's problems, strengths, plans, operations, goals, past successes, and past failures. There may even be information available on the company's hiring practices. This will let you orient your statements to its needs and also establish that you've done some homework and know what you're talking about.

Getting across these three points is your primary objective in any interview. No matter what the interviewer wants to talk about, you want that person to hear what you can do, how well you can do it (or how well you've done it in the past), and how your skill and experience relate to and can benefit that company. Don't let any questions, comments, ramblings, or war stories distract you from making your points. Even if the interviewer asks the wrong questions, you can give the right answers. I have to stress this point because most interviewers are not good interviewers. You won't always be given an opportunity to tell your story as you'd planned, so you may have to create that opportunity. This isn't usually maliciousness on the interviewer's part but rather ineptness. My advice is to never leave an interview without having made your best case—unless, of course, you've lost all interest in the job that's available.

Using all the tact, charm, and subtlety you can muster, you have to take control of the interview, always allowing the interviewer to continue to feel in control. You must keep returning to what you can do, how well you can do it, and how that might apply to the interviewer's needs. Don't linger over a general conversation. Keep the spotlight focused on the subject of the interview—you.

THE WAY THE GAME IS PLAYED

There are two kinds of interviews, the general interview and the specific job interview.

The general interview is aimed at establishing and developing leads. You want someone of some consequence to know that you're available and have something to offer. It may turn out that this contact does become interested in hiring you. So much the better. But otherwise your attitude is "I'm not expecting you to offer me a job. Rather, I'd like to explore with you where someone with my background and skills might be useful to someone in your field or someone you know who might be interested." This immediately lowers the interviewer's resistance. He's off the hook and only being asked for advice and possible leads. He doesn't have to face the problem of turning down another nice person and is flattered into being in a position we all love, that of expert. It also opens the door to his hearing a straightforward presentation of your skills and experience. How can he make a suggestion to you or advise someone with your background without learning what that background is?

There are two possible outcomes to this sort of interview—it becomes an actual job interview (with the discovery of what a wonderful addition you would be to his team) or you turn it into leads to other interviews. There is, of course, a third possibility—a dead-end failure—but that's likely to be your own fault. Even here, guilt and time wasting may be avoided simply by pressing for other leads. "Who else do you think I might talk to to explore other possibilities in my field?" Get names, titles, and other information to the extent that you can without being pushy. Ideally, you may even impress your interviewer enough that he'll volunteer to telephone his leads on your behalf and let them know they'll be hearing from you.

Door opening of this sort is devoutly to be wished if not actively pursued. Your contact can hardly call his friend or associate on your behalf without saying something favorable about you. Your ultimate objective here is to create a network of contacts who are familiar with your abilities, who are impressed by your credentials and by you, and who know you're available. Remember, more good jobs come through such networks than through the want ads. A friend, or a friend of a friend, can be an invaluable lead to the right job.

If your general interview becomes a job interview, it means you've done well and can shift gears. The job interview usually has a predictable structure:

- You describe your background and skills.
- The interviewer describes the job.
- You relate your skills and experience to the job.
- If the interviewer becomes seriously interested in you, then it is your turn to interview him or her in detail about the job. Find out what you can about the responsibilities, authority, opportunity, job description and flexibility, budget, supervisor, staff and associates, company standards and expectations, resources, procedures, personalities, prospects for the future, and anything else that might be relevant to you.
- You and the interviewer discuss salary, benefits, amenities, and other details.
- Intermission. Rarely is a job offered, or accepted, on the spot. Both parties need additional time to think about it. The interviewer will check your references. You'll look over the company materials and publications. Often other interviews will occur during this break.
- Offer and acceptance. More discussion and exchange of information. Anything to be further negotiated regarding salary, perks, vacation, and the like are hashed out here. Then the decision is made by both parties.

PERFORMING EFFECTIVELY

Although the circumstances may be slightly different, the job interview, like any speaking situation, is essentially a matter of communication—the way you present yourself and your ideas, and the way they are perceived by your audience, in this case the interviewer. So naturally the same techniques and strategies apply in both situations. If you've mastered the use of your face, your gestures, and your voice; if you're prepared and confident; if you send the winning signals in the way you look and the way you dress, you can master any job interview that comes your way.

One final piece of advice: A job interview can be, and often is, a kind of mini-confrontation, and an interviewer, like an aggressive reporter, may ask you questions that are difficult, if not impossible, to answer. But you can turn negative questions into positive answers. Pause, look at the interviewer, and then give honest, positive answers that will present you in the best possible light. So if your interviewer zings you with "What do you consider your greatest weakness?" if it's the truth try "Most of the people I work with think I'm too dedicated to my job." Or "My attention to detail seems to bother some colleagues, but usually not the boss." If you're asked "What's the minimum salary you'll accept," don't be afraid to toss it back: "I think I should be offered whatever salary the job is worth to the company. What figure did you have in mind?"

"What's the biggest mistake you've made professionally?" Turn it around: "I once trusted a person more than I should have. His actions hurt me and my business associates. It taught me to check people out."

"Don't you honestly believe you're overqualified for this position?" If you believe the interviewer's perception is wrong, you might try "Not unless you've got a lid on the job, the salary, and the responsibility that I'm not aware of."

A job interview is a one-on-one situation, and just as the interviewer is sizing you up by the signals you send, you can size up the company by carefully observing *his* signals. Is he open, considerate, courteous? Or closed, uninterested, harsh, or even hostile? It won't take you long to figure that one out. And if the latter, you'd probably rather not work for the company he represents. In fact, *he* may soon be out of a job.

WINNING

MEETING

TECHNIQUES

Meetings are the staple of the American business diet. If you could grow good ones, you'd make a fortune. And if you could make every meeting productive, you'd be acclaimed a wizard—nothing less than a Merlin.

Every meeting has its natural barriers to success:

Poor facilities
Technical equipment breakdowns
Uncomfortable surroundings
Boring people
Bad planning
Dull speakers
Bad refreshments
Unskilled chairmen
Lack of direction
Digressions from the agenda
Professional troublemakers in attendance
Unfunny jesters
Unessential interruptions to prove someone's importance

The list is endless, but the fact remains that meetings are the most frequent way in which we communicate with our colleagues and coworkers, our superiors and subordinates. If meetings fail, there has been a failure of communication.

Why should a meeting be different from any other speaking situation? It isn't. Someone talks and others listen. There are hundreds of reasons for a meeting's failure. But there's only one reason why a meeting is successful—something specific was accomplished and everyone in the room knew it and went away better off for it. Usually, the person in the front of the room, the person in charge of the meeting, the chief speaker, is primarily responsible for the outcome. But words alone do not a successful meeting make. Skillful, dynamic presentations do, whether you are the chairman, the chief speaker, or a participant. The way you present yourself and your ideas, the way you communicate, can make all the difference between just getting through a meeting and getting the results you hoped for.

You know the difference I'm talking about. We've all been sorry we had to attend many of the meetings we've gone to, and we've been to a few that really excited us. The meetings we left feeling that something had really been accomplished usually had an exciting, outstanding, dynamic chairperson. Compelling. Spellbinding. A person who reached us on a personal, intellectual, and emotional level. Was that person a natural? Was there some special genius? Maybe, but probably not. Most of the really skilled communicators got where they are by working at developing their speaking skills.

As with all speaking skills, meeting skills can be acquired. More than that, they *must* be acquired. Today's work environment assigns more and more of us the task of opening our mouths in front of colleagues. We give reports, briefings, instructions, and introductions. We serve on or we chair committees and task forces. We participate in meetings, seminars, and workshops. And in every one of these scenarios, we're expected to be active participants—to speak up.

▪ WHY ME?

The 1977 best-seller *The Book of Lists* included a category called The Fourteen Worst Human Fears. Fear number one was speaking before a group, death was *sixth*. And of all speaking situations, the ones with the most riding on them are the professional ones. So colleagues, peers, bosses, and fellow professionals become the enemy. We're so petrified by the fear of failure that we close up, tighten up, and do all the wrong things. We tend to let stress overcome us rather than overcoming stress.

Instead of attacking the problems, we often succumb to them. We know we're out of our league being expected to conduct a dynamic meeting. Our hyperactive imaginations scream our inadequacies: "I'm not good enough," "I'll really louse up and they'll laugh at me," "The boss won't think I'm authoritative enough." We produce an endless list of reasons why we may fail, including, "I'll be so nervous I'll forget to zip my fly."

Notice that the focus is turned inward, on themselves. We see ourselves through the magnifying glass of fear and confusion. Every misplaced hair makes us think, "I look like the Ayatollah." Our deep-seated anxieties set off all kinds of alarms. Our confidence, if we ever had any, disappears. We envision being publicly exposed as dumb, phony, wrong, inadequate, incompetent, and worse. We're stark naked in a meeting room filled with fully clothed people.

While this scenario may seem exaggerated for some people, it's no less true for others. We look upon ourselves and see the worst. We forget that when we're the audience we don't look at other front-of-the-room speakers in the same searching, scorching light. There's the key to overcoming our fear—that and breathing to relax and regain control of ourselves.

The truth is that the audience doesn't care about the things you may consider physical imperfections. They will accept you as you are. Yes, you should look your best. Of course you should dress neatly and inconspicuously. But your colleagues aren't looking at your weight or your hair or your nose or teeth. If they know you, they're used to seeing you as you really are, warts and all. If they don't know you, they may take a quick inventory of your appearance and leave it at that, unless you begin to bore them. In other words, self-consciousness is a self-centered waste of good energy. What the attendees *do* care about is your performance. That's where your concern and energy ought to be directed.

As in any speaking situation, your audience will give you from the very outset the benefit of the doubt. The chairman is expected to be the chairman. The invited speaker must have something to share. The report-giver is presumed to know the project being reported on. More than that, the group *wants* the chairman to be effective, the speaker to be interesting and informative, the instructor to be knowledgeable. In short, audiences invest the person with the qualities that go with his role. This phenomenon is a tremendous asset to you. The group quite matter-of-factly assumes that you know what you're about. For their attitude to change, you've got to *prove them wrong*. Conversely, if you perform more or less as they expect, you confirm their expectations and strengthen their acceptance of you.

What this means is that you can step out of yourself and into a speaker's role with the support and encouragement of the group. Act otherwise and you lose support automatically. And be aware that these attitudes are created not by who you are, they're born of self-interest. People don't want to waste their time or be bored, they want the meeting to go well for their own sakes. This automatically spells support for you and you can count on it. On the other hand, if you're preoccupied with yourself rather than the group and the event, you'll soon feel the positive vibrations converting to the sort of negative energy that causes cold sweat and a longing for oblivion. So forget yourself. Concentrate on your role. Remember all communication is sharing ideas, an intellectual act of love. You can't give yourself totally to your audience when your concentration is on yourself.

Many of us are reluctant to play a role. We don't want to be considered actors. If we do, our audience will think we're phonies. At the same time, we fear that our real selves will automatically be rejected. Both visions are false. The underlying reason for every successful public performance is the communicator's ability to, at least partially, forget about self and imagined shortcomings and to concentrate on the event, his role in it, and the audience he's delivering to. It's the trademark of all successful communication. Remember that and you'll succeed. Worry about hair out of place and you'll fulfill your fear of failure.

ᴿWHAT DOES THE GROUP EXPECT?

Leadership is the first quality. From chairpersons, discussion leaders, speakers, and instructors, the group wants leadership. During your time as chairman or speaker, you're presiding. You're the one in charge. You have the right to control what happens and the obligation to see that it's effective. Sins against good leadership include:

Lack of control
Lack of preparation
Rambling or boring presentations
Indecisiveness
Vagueness
Disorganization
Unclear objectives
Lack of sensitivity to the needs and wants of the group
Running overtime

Implicit in the list is the harsh fact that the person up front must know what he or she is doing and do it well. So make your presentation with warmth, authority, and assurance. Do it efficiently and effectively. Do it on behalf of the audience and be responsive to its needs and interests. This isn't said to intimidate or to frighten the newcomer but to emphasize the need for competence in the speaking skills talked about throughout this book. Cockiness is no less doomed to failure than a publicly displayed inferiority complex. You have a responsibility to your audience to know how to do your job well and to be responsive to the people present. If I had to select the two items that destroy most meetings, I'd choose dull presiders and lack of sensitivity to the needs and wants of the group.

Content—real meat, not watery gruel—is the substance of your presentation. The virtues of a good presentation include:

Solid information
Reliable data
Logical organization
Plain language

Sharply etched conclusions and recommendations
Examples relevant to the group's experience
Clear direction and purpose
An opportunity for the group to question and discuss what's
   been said
A chance for the group to get something of value for itself

Skill and style, the way you present yourself and your ideas, is
no less important than what you have to say. The way you speak,
move, act and react; the way you relate to the group—all can
spell success or failure for the meeting. In a more formal situation,
there's usually a certain distance between you and your audience.
In a meeting, that distance is considerably diminished and, from
the moment you walk into the room until the moment you walk
out, you're *on*.

THE MEETING AS COMMUNICATION

Basically, there are five types of meetings, most of which have
overlapping functions and purposes.

- Information Meetings: These are intended to deliver or exchange
  information. The boss has announcements to make. A federal
  agency wants to tell interested parties about up-coming regu-
  lations. The CEO expects the department heads to brief each
  other on the recent progress and plans for the next calendar
  period. A manager wants to exchange thoughts with other
  managers.
- Decision-Making Meetings: These are meetings in which a
  group negotiates or builds a concensus in order to arrive at a
  decision.
- Instruction Meetings: These include training and educational
  programs of all kinds, meetings to issue directives and assign-
  ments, and events intended to result in change or action on
  the part of the participants.

- Motivation Meetings: People's hearts and minds have to be won. They must be moved to respond. Buy this soap. Stop smoking. Improve your sales by learning these new techniques. Use these manuals and do better. Give us your support. Join our team. Whatever the subject area, these are meetings to persuade, cajole, motivate, inspire, induce a desired action.
- Social Meetings: If there is a meeting that's purely social, it's often held to reward certain team members for exceptional performance. But more often than not, the annual meeting or the team meeting is held with the social aspect as just one of its purposes. The Internal Revenue Service has seen to that by requiring an organization to have some official business purpose for any portion of the meeting that it claims as tax deductible.

Almost every meeting you attend combines one or several of the five purposes. But whatever its purpose, the success or failure of the meeting depends upon the success or failure of the communication between the members of the group. Conceive of meetings as communication and you'll begin to think of them in a new and productive light. Whatever other role you are asked to play, you have to function as a communicator. No other concept of yourself—executive, taxpayer, expert, supervisor, professional—is half so pertinent and essential as the fact that you are a *communicator*.

No ONE HAS THE RIGHT TO BE DULL

Statistics show that most professionals spend more than 50 percent of their work time in meetings. Some sources cite a figure more like 65 percent. And among professionals it is almost unanimous that most meetings they attend have been a waste of time. Why? Because their leaders or speakers failed to communicate. What a colossal waste of everybody's time!

People who go to meetings offer us their time and attention. They often pay for the privilege of attending. They almost always leave important work behind. They deserve genuine efforts at professionalism in platform behavior. No one has the right to be dull for *any* reason—not because of greater importance or a busy schedule, not because of expertise superior to the audience's, and not even because of shyness or lack of skill. As Jack Mannion of the American Water Works Foundation said, "If speakers are not willing to make the effort necessary to achieve at least a modicum of good technique and authentic communication, they have no right to the platform."

Whether you are the leader or a speaker, to give the attendees what they deserve requires the techniques as described in Part I of this book—style, skill, preparation, and confidence. But, as a leader, you have additional responsibilities. A meeting can't just happen by itself simply because a group of people has assembled at your invitation or command. You have to plan everything from "Good morning" down to "This meeting is adjourned." You have to make sure the technical details work. You have to have and stick to an agenda. To put it into English, you have to know what you want to get done and do it. And you have to start on time and keep the meeting moving so that you can end it on schedule. You've got to know the ideas you want to communicate and the best way to deliver them. But apart from that, a number of other factors, and how well you've thought them through, will determine the success or failure of the meeting.

THE SITE

Comfort and convenience should determine your choice of site. And remember, as soon as you move out of your office, your board room, or another facility in your headquarters, you're on foreign soil. That's true even if you're in a hotel where you've had lots of previous meetings, a friend's office where you've been dozens of times, or a local school auditorium or classroom where you've held meetings before. Something about the off-premises site or the personnel working there is different. You need to plan for the inevitable surprises. If you need a lectern, a microphone, a flip chart, a projector, *anything*, make sure it's there, it works, and that you and your technician have rehearsed with it. That may seem so basic that it hardly deserves mention, but we've all been to meetings where "no problem" became famous last words.

When I conduct one of my training sessions, I'm in the room where my program is scheduled at least an hour before starting time with the video operator. My equipment list was in my client's possession along with the contract for my services. The meeting planner and my assistant have spoken many times. When necessary, we've been in touch with the site staff in advance. Microphones, recorders, video playbacks? The more complicated the equipment you plan to use, the more there is that can go wrong. The message is simply this: No amount of checking is too much. Take absolutely nothing for granted. But don't panic when something does go wrong. If the attendees aren't aware of a problem, there isn't any. There may be some grief and anxiety for you and the technical staff, but as long as the audience isn't aware of it, the program has a better chance for success.

THE OCCASION

The occasion obviously influences your choice of site and the way you conduct a meeting. For a small informal meeting or lunch, choose the appropriate setting and encourage everyone to participate. The success of a large meeting depends a lot on the total control by the chairperson, without the audience being aware of its lack of participation. Whatever the occasion, your audience will have expectations that you must meet.

THE PURPOSE

The reason for your meeting determines how and where it takes place. Make sure all three factors work together. An auditorium may be appropriate for information and instruction meetings but not for decision-making and social meetings. You can't expect to build a meaningful consensus toward making an important decision at a cocktail party, nor can you expect colleagues and coworkers to get to know each other better if you don't give them the time and the freedom to do so.

THE NUMBER AND TYPES OF ATTENDEES

Again, this depends on the purpose of the meeting, but a good rule is the smaller the group, the harder your job. The danger is that the bigger the meeting, the more formal we tend to make it. Formal, yes, if necessary. But pompous, no. You and your speakers must remember to make your presentations as close to one-on-one talks as possible. Don't make speeches. Don't preach, orate, or teach. *Talk* to your audience. And while the number and the "types" of people in attendance may influence what you have to say, your delivery should remain exactly the same.

THE NUMBER OF SPEAKERS, PRESENTERS, INSTRUCTORS, INTRODUCERS

The more of them, the harder your job, and, obviously, the more attention you need to pay to details. A few notes might help. Discourage the use of slides, charts, graphs, overhead projections, and other visual aids, especially in large meeting rooms. The people who sit in the back have a hard enough time seeing the speaker, let alone a lot of mechanical devices. And when you light a room for slides, the speaker is very often left in the dark. I believe a speaker is his own best visual aid. A really dynamite presenter doesn't need so-called help. My rule is this: Unless the visual tells your story better than you can, scrap it. A picture may be worth a thousand words, but when it doesn't do a thing for the audience's understanding, a visual aid becomes a cop-out and a distraction.

Watch out, too, for the "introduction trap." We feel that every speaker needs to have his whole life story told to the audience. Wrong. The shorter the better, providing two qualifications are met: The audience should be eager to hear this person based on your introduction, and the speaker should be made proud to have been invited.

The most powerful introduction today is "Ladies and gentlemen, the President of the United States." Imagine how foolish it would sound to hear "And now, ladies and gentlemen, a man who was a B-movie actor for many years, a former liberal labor leader who changed his political affiliation, became governor of California . . ."

I've had the misfortune to have the presiding officer "read" my bio in detail. Yet after the program people still asked, "What did you do before you became a speech consultant?" It was all said, but nobody heard. Then there are the times when the introducer will say, "Last March I saw our speaker do a training session and said, 'We've got to bring him to our meeting.' I got the best information I've ever received at a convention program, and I'm certain you'll say the same. So please welcome our speaker, Arch Lustberg." He made the audience want to hear me. He made me feel proud to be there. It took about ten seconds. It couldn't have been better.

CONTINUITY

Even the most carefully planned meeting can still wander off course without the proper leadership *during* the meeting. Here are some tips to keep your meetings *on* course:

- Start on time. Don't punish promptness.
- Have a wonderful welcome ready. If you haven't been able to greet everyone personally at the door because of the sheer numbers, be sure to prepare a warm, friendly, sincere welcome.

- State the objective of the meeting. Even if the group has a detailed published agenda, briefly cover the highlights.
- Get everyone involved. Encourage participation. Even in large meetings this can be done by requesting the attendees to fill out questionnaires.
- Ask leading questions. Call on silent types but don't embarrass them. Sidestep the domineering talkers.
- Tie agenda items together. Provide links from one point to another. Offer periodic summaries.
- Venture tentative conclusions or agreements. Submit them as your understanding of what's been said so far for the group's approval.
- Watch for nonverbal signals. If you sense disapproval, strong agreement, boredom, skepticism, objections, call for comment.
- Be nonjudgmental. You are the moderator, the traffic cop. Lead the group toward your desired objective but don't try to dictate the outcome.
- Keep on time. Keep the subject matter on track. Without appearing rude, cut through digressions and irrelevancies.
- Communicate your genuine respect for the members of the group and what they have to say. This established, they'll tolerate and support your efforts to control digressions and other roadblocks and work with rather than against you to achieve the desired objective.
- End on time. Even better, end early.

Consider some additional tips. Force yourself to listen. Concentrate. Pay attention. Don't anticipate what's coming next. Above all, don't finish other people's sentences, no matter how slowly or deliberately they speak. Ask questions. Be sure you understand what's just been said and make sure the group understands what you're saying.

If you're open and honest and put into practice all the other rules and techniques of good communication, you'll encourage everyone else in the group to do the same. As the leader of a meeting, or as a participant when it's your turn to speak, remember you're the spark plug that keeps the engine running and the meeting on course toward its desired destination. A friend gave me a wonderful thought to share with you: "Maybe there's no spark in the organization if there's no spark in the meeting."

WINNING
TEACHING
TECHNIQUES

Teachers, like all those who speak to others as part of their jobs, often forget that the prime purpose of the teaching profession is *communication*. Teachers often forget this within weeks of the first semester on the job because they must deal with a lot of externals that seem to have very little to do with communicating.

▪THE TEACHER AS ADMINISTRATOR

If you're a teacher, no sooner do you report to work than you're faced with the realization that a teacher is not *just* a teacher. The job description says teacher, but you're also warden, shrink, surrogate parent, traffic cop, records keeper (attendance taker, grade recorder, paper grader, administrative flunky), messenger, cafeteria security guard, and about a dozen other people.

The overwhelming responsibilities of the nonclassroom, nonteaching aspects of the work may obscure your focus as a teacher. What was to have been a job you really looked forward to starts to look like a nightmare of extraneous responsibilities. I know. I've been there.

Don't lose sight of the fact that *teaching* is your first priority, and teaching demands skillful communication techniques.

▪THE TEACHER AS COMMUNICATOR

Every dictionary synonym for *teach* suggests a receiver for the information being taught by the teacher—impart, direct, instruct, inform, educate, inculcate, enlighten, indoctrinate, train. The video operator for a California program I conducted put it this way: "The great teachers are the great storytellers." I couldn't agree more. Or to put it another way: Students are members of an audience.

A teacher is in the classroom for one primary reason—to give information. *Give* is the key word here. It isn't enough to know your subject. It isn't enough to be a great source of information. The secret to really good teaching is good communication, the ability to get the information from your mind into the student's mind. That takes a dynamic delivery. It requires the skills of the open face and the gesture. It requires the ability to look and sound like the most important thing in your life at this particular moment is this communication. The same rule applies to teaching as to any other speaking situation—*no one has the right to be dull.* I'm not saying you have to be a good entertainer to teach (though it certainly never hurt), but at the very least, you *must* be interesting.

Ironically, one of the pitfalls of teaching is familiarity with your subject. After a while, teaching can become as routine as small talk. But what may be tiresome to you after you've been over the same material dozens of times is still brand new to the student. This is the one point you must never forget.

In the theater, actors are told about the "illusion of the first time" and taught the techniques they need to achieve this freshness. This is simply the ability to make the audience believe that you're telling this story, saying these words, communicating these ideas for the first time and spontaneously. It's a vital part of acting because every performance after opening night is a repeat, but it should still be as fresh and interesting as it was the first time.

Why has no one ever stressed that same notion with teaching? It deserves consideration. Every Algebra I class is essentially the same as every other Algebra I class. The teacher needs to keep the image of the "first time" in his or her presentation in order to make the material fresh and interesting for the students, who in fact are hearing it for the first time.

Most of us are what we are and have certain academic strengths and weaknesses because a particular group of teachers excited us and another group turned us off. A good teacher must have a tremendous desire and an excellent ability to get the message across to the student. Dull teachers can make a bore out of exciting material, but interesting teachers, good teachers, can make magic out of what would otherwise be very ordinary material. Perhaps it would help if the designation *teacher* were given only to those who were interesting in the front of the classroom and a different name given to those who merely presented material by rote.

It might seem like a revolutionary idea, but think of what a difference it would make in our ability to educate if all teachers were required to develop good communication skills in addition to their academic requirements. It happened to me and I'm sure it's happened to you. There were times when going to school was a joy. And there were other times when you were literally sick before the school bell rang at the start of the day. The difference was almost always in the teacher's ability to create interest and enthusiasm in the classroom, no matter what the subject.

If the material is boring to the teacher, it will be boring to the class, but the converse isn't necessarily true. Just because the teacher is interested in the material, it doesn't necessarily mean the class will be interested. The responsibility of the teacher is to get the class interested. This means making the classroom an exciting place to be in. It also means that each day's lesson has to be presented in the most interesting, pleasant, vital, exciting manner possible. When viewed in this light, teaching can be one of the most challenging and rewarding careers anyone could choose.

I did a training program for the teachers of a major school system in the Southwest. It took place the day before the fall term was to begin in that particular area. There were 1,200 teachers attending the program. Two participants had prepared to present their opening-day classes in front of the group and knew they were to be videotaped. Each one greeted us as though we were the class and did the first five minutes of the lecture. Before playing back the videotape to show them how they came across, I talked about the speaking techniques that make for great communication: open face, open body, voice, preparation, confidence, delivery. Then we played back their demonstrations, watching them in the light of those techniques. Both participants, along with the audience, saw the strengths they should keep and the weaknesses they should eliminate.

Then the two participants delivered the same opening a second time. The difference seemed like magic. The second time around, they made a conscious effort to open their faces. They gestured on their descriptive words. They were alive. They were dynamic. They were dramatic. They made intellectual love to us. Everyone was so delighted that they gave the two participants a standing ovation to express their pleasure with the improvement in their teaching skills.

And here's what everyone in the audience learned about good teachers:

- They should leave their nonteaching responsibilities behind.
- They should remember that the student has never heard any of this before.
- They should make an event out of the class.
- If they enjoyed themselves, their students would enjoy themselves—and learn.
- Above all, they could get more attention and have greater impact if they stopped thinking about themselves as disciplinarians and remembered that their function is communication.

Again, if whoever is in the front of the room isn't communicating, that person is not a teacher. The same goes for the pulpit. If whoever is up there isn't communicating, that person's not a preacher.

In the sense of communicating information, every speaker in every situation is a teacher, whose primary responsibility is not to himself but to his audience. That's why I like to think of speaking not merely as a teaching process, but as a learning process too.

WINNING

NEGOTIATING

TECHNIQUES

The dictionary defines the verb *negotiate* as "To confer with another in bargaining or trade. To hold conference and discussion with a view to reaching agreement on contract." Nowhere does it say that negotiation must involve argument, tantrums, hostility, animosity, hatred. But unfortunately, that's the meaning management–labor disputes and acrimonious lawsuits have given the word.

Yet, in truth, every time you buy a product, you've negotiated; you've reached agreement on a contract. The dealer put a price tag on his product and you decided to buy it or not. There may be some room for further negotiations over price, terms, time of delivery, etc., but in the end you either buy the product or you don't. So ends every negotiation—a decision is made. If it's a good deal for both parties, the negotiation ends successfully. If it isn't a good deal, it doesn't. That's the perfect negotiation. It begins, it ends, and everyone is satisfied that the right decision has been made.

But there are very few opportunities for perfect negotiations left. In most of our everyday transactions, the terms are set with no room for negotiation. And when there is negotiating room, the situation is often turned into a confrontation.

We've already seen that in such adversarial situations if only one person wins, *both* lose. In contract talks, in family arguments, in *all* imperfect negotiation situations, it's vital to realize that if both sides receive fair treatment, both sides come out winners. If you take unfair advantage of the other side in order to win, ultimately *you* lose.

We all want to win. That's become the nature of competition, and from an early age we've learned all kinds of tricks and tactics, some good, some bad, to get what we want. Among the bad ones are:

Constant argument, until the other side gives in	Intimidation
	Aggravation
	Cheating
Tantrums	Lying

Some of the good ones are:

Logic	Analysis
Reason	Common sense

And remember that the only successful negotiation is the one
in which there are *two winners*. When there are two winners, each
comes out with self-esteem intact. No one needs to feel subser-
vient, beaten, put upon, a loser.

It's almost inevitable that in imperfect negotiations we develop
a lot of stress. Stress is a natural reaction to any out-of-the-
ordinary situation, but you mustn't let it dominate you. If you let
it take over, it develops into anger, hostility, personal animosity,
or even irrational behavior. It controls the negotiation, blocks
out logic, reason, and common sense. The possibility of compromise goes down the tube.

When the situation seems to be getting out of hand, when it
becomes impossible to like your adversary, when there seems to
be absolutely no merit to the other side's point of view, when
your adversary seems subhuman to you, when you're tempted to
shout and scream, when everything gets personal and seems in-
sulting—break off for a while. Call time out. You need a cooling-
off period. Or if you really believe and agree that you're never
going to get together, call off the negotiation.

If you do elect to try to keep things going after a break,
remember a few simple principles:

You can't throw a tantrum with your mouth shut.
You can't scream, yell, or holler when you're smiling.
You can't fly off the handle with your brows elevated.

Some golden rules of negotiating:

- Listen.
- Talk about relevant issues that involve the present.
- Avoid past problems.
- Talk about the possible.
- Avoid the impossible, or the unlikely.
- Start with those issues likely to lend themselves to early solu-
tions.

- Stick to the agenda items; avoid digressions and detours.
- If an impasse looks likely, table that issue and move on to the next one.
- Watch and be alert and sensitive to timing. If you sense the time is right for agenda item number four, skip right to it.
- Be courteous; avoid put-downs, insults, insinuations, and sarcasm. If you must use humor, make it self-deprecating. Don't make fun of the other guy; be sensitive to his wants and needs.
- Think and talk alternatives.
- Think and talk creative solutions. Don't get locked into "doing it this way because that's the way we've always done it."

I have an interesting theory. When it seems impossible to resolve a conflict, when the screaming begins, when the other side is dead wrong and you're obviously right (and convinced that even your adversary knows you're right)—try *apologizing*. Your overwrought adversary can't. So don't tell the other side it is wrong. It already knows it.

A POSITIVE BEGINNING

Usually, we start a negotiation with what each side "demands," wants, or expects. I suggest that each side sift through the other's demands immediately, then go immediately to what's possible. That seems revolutionary, but it can really cut out a lot of the usual garbage. Are there any areas of give and take that can serve as the real starting point? In other words, use the opening moments of a negotiation to sort out the points on the table to find areas of potential agreement rather than starting with the areas of extreme disagreement.
Some helpful questions to ask:

What do we want in common?
What can we achieve that would put each of us in a somewhat more advantageous position?

What does each party contribute to the success of the other?
Where can we compromise?

Questions to avoid:

What can I con them out of?
What can I do or say to get an edge?
What can I do to intimidate them?
What do they owe me?
How am I superior and how can I flaunt that?
Don't they realize I can exist without them?
Why isn't the other side grateful for all I've done for them?

WHAT ARE OUR OPTIONS?

Openly examine the consequences if I give you everything you're
asking for. Then turn it around and examine the consequences if
you give me everything I want. A lot of problems can be avoided
if we understand how extreme the extremes really are. Then we
can move into what solutions might work for both sides if compromise is possible. And never forget one basic principle—some
"posturing" may be necessary in your camp or in the opponent's
camp in order to keep the "troops" happy. But each of you should
be prepared to acknowledge and accept it as part of the negotiating process. It's remarkable that after a long, acrimonious
strike, as the settlement is announced, each side feels obliged to
talk about how good the contract is, how happy both sides are
with the settlement, and how much this means to everyone involved. Why, oh why, couldn't they have gotten there before
the strike?

I vividly remember an adversarial contract negotiation I was
involved in many years ago. At least it seemed adversarial to me
because I didn't understand that I was part of a "game" being
played by two opposing attorneys. Each side wanted to reach an

agreement. Each side saw terrific possibilities arising from the proposed relationship. Lots of the details had been hammered out between the attorneys on the telephone before this meeting ever took place. In fact, the contracts were drafted, and supposedly all that remained was for the signing to take place. My attorney and I flew from New York to Chicago to "finalize" the deal. Three hours after the meeting began, the lawyers were shouting at each other. The final numbers were conflicting. My attorney slammed shut his attaché case, said angrily, "Come on, Arch, we're walking," and stormed out.

I had no idea what I was supposed to do. I'd never been involved in a contract negotiation like this before. So I followed like a newborn calf. By the time we reached the receptionist's desk, my lawyer winked at me as the other attorneys called us back into the conference room, and we finalized the deal within minutes. It was the "obligatory scene." It was the expected tantrum. It was high drama.

I hope those days of contract negotiations are over, but I fear not. That was the way those particular attorneys felt they were getting an "edge" for their client. I felt all along that the same result could have been reached several hours earlier if the negotiating concept involved what was right for each side. But then again, attorneys are paid by the hour.

Try to remember:

Fair beats unfair.
Justice beats injustice.

My attorney admitted to me on the plane ride home that we had achieved exactly what he thought we'd achieve, and he was really proud of having achieved it. That was fine for me, but I wondered how many other deals have been blown away by unnecessary histrionics. I now consider those tactics barbaric. The notion of courtesy, fairness, justice should never take second place to a victory that annihilates the "opposition."

▪NEGOTIATION AS COMMUNICATION

In the ideal negotiation, both sides take turns expressing their ideas and exchanging information. In other words, this is a speaking situation. And because it is also confrontational, it requires the utmost in speaking skills. To relax and overcome stress, breathe properly. To get your points across with honesty and conviction, speak with an open face and appropriate gestures. Be prepared. Be confident. Be courteous. Be yourself. And search for ways to be allies rather than enemies. The statesman seeks solutions. The general seeks supremacy. Be a statesman rather than a general.

WINNING

SALES

TECHNIQUES

Just as we're all negotiators every day and we're all teachers every day, we're all salespeople constantly. Every time we speak, we're selling ourselves. Every time we open our mouths, we're selling our ideas. There's not a lot of difference when you're selling an actual product, but there are some special considerations.

Selling is the process of persuading a person or a group to buy a product or a service. The more beneficial to both, the more likely it is that the sale will be made and, more important, that each party will come away satisfied with the transaction. For a sale to happen and for customer satisfaction to be the final and enduring result, some basic principles apply.

First, you've got to know your product. You've got to know it thoroughly and speak about it with confidence and authority. You also have to know the competition thoroughly. This allows you to speak well of your competition while emphasizing your own strengths.

Second, you have to believe in your company, your product, and yourself. You have to be proud to represent your company. It's obviously the best in its field. After all, it hired *you*.

Third, "Ya' gotta know the territory," as Meredith Willson said in one of the songs from *The Music Man*. That means you need to know who is the decision-maker and sell to that person. It's a total waste of time to make the sale and then discover that you have to make it again because you've been selling to the wrong person. I realize that sometimes you have to do it twice, but if once will do, why repeat?

THE THREE I's

To accomplish these three steps, the good salesperson must have and exercise what salesman Steve Niven calls "The Three I's":

> Intelligence
> Integrity
> Initiative

By intelligence, we're not talking about a high IQ. We're talking about sensitivity, timing, friendliness, warmth, and solid *information*.

Integrity is the hallmark of the salesperson who has long-term success. Yes, a lot of fly-by-night people make megabucks at other people's expense, but the customers of a salesperson with real integrity keep coming back because they know they'll get honesty, quality, price, and service. A person can't have just a little integrity. It's something you either have or you don't. And that's what the customer becomes aware of very early in the selling game. You have to have a good name, and the only way you get that and keep it is by having integrity.

Initiative is the ability to get in the door, to make the presentation in a unique, interesting, imaginative way, and to know you did a good job for yourself and the company even if you didn't make the sale.

▪SELLING AS COMMUNICATION

Why should selling a product be any different from selling yourself or your ideas? It isn't. A company is only as good as the people who represent it, and for the moment you're the company. And, in almost every case, the client has to believe in *you* before believing in what you're selling. So, what should the client see?

A warm person
A sincere person
An open person
An enthusiastic person
A trustworthy person

The client also wants a positive person. He wants you to tell him the good features of your product, *not* to bad-mouth the competition. If there were problems in the past, don't blame the home office or the shipping department, just take the initiative and be sure it doesn't happen again or you can kiss that account goodbye. Don't make claims or promises that can't be kept. If you are the best and if you represent the best, your client will get what he buys, he'll get it on time, he'll be happy with it, and he'll welcome anything you bring him in the future.

Don't be discouraged by a series of "no sale" calls. You can't know why you didn't make the sale, and sometimes it has nothing to do with you, your product, or your presentation. If you suspect it's you, then work at improving your selling techniques. But don't lose sight of other factors that may have caused the buyer to look elsewhere. It's not outside the realm of belief in today's world that someone is "kicking back." The buyer may have a brother-in-law selling the same basic products. You may be dealing with a true status quo person: "We've been buying Faunce Corporation's widgets for thirty years and we're happy with them." There are reasons you'll never even dream of, so just press on, improve, grow, and do the best you can.

Time is an important commodity. Don't waste it. When you're making a sale, know all your facts. State them. Answer any questions. Ask for the order. Thank your client. Go.

Vary your presentations. Keep them fresh. Use your imagination. Be creative. Dare to be different. This sets you apart from the pack and will help you make the sale.

Enjoy your work. Believe it or not, it's contagious. Just as when you make intellectual love to your audience, your audience loves you back, when you're having a good time working, it shows and other people enjoy your enjoyment.

I remember watching Ed McMahon, my favorite salesman, selling vegetable slicers the way he had done it years before on the Boardwalk in Atlantic City. It was such great fun for him that people who didn't need slicers, who didn't even *want* slicers, bought them to show that they enjoyed his enjoyment. It was their way of applauding him for a great show. Now, you may not be selling slicers, but you are putting on a show for your client, so a key ingredient is the ability to have a good time doing it.

In all the seminars I've conducted, the technique I teach that was most helpful to salespeople was the technique of the open face. Even the most successful salespeople in those sessions agreed that they had found a new clue to helping them be believed, trusted, and, ultimately, even more successful. I urge you to work on this technique every chance you get. Your mirror may not buy what you have to sell but your clients and customers will.

THE
COMPLETE
SPEAKER'S
HANDBOOK

Here is a summary of the major communication skills and techniques that you'll find helpful for a quick review before any speaking assignment. Let's begin with the things I urge you to do.

Throw out anything I've suggested that isn't comfortable for you. It's important to appear natural to your audience. If a technique feels fake, it will probably look fake. *But* before you decide to discard a suggestion, *try it out.* You may find new freedom, new naturalness, new skill. The open face and the gesture come to mind immediately. You may think you're looking stupid, foolish, and "bug-eyed" when, really, you may be barely elevating those brows. One client told me, "I must never gesture. People are constantly telling me I look like a windmill." I suggested that he continue to use gestures but make a conscious effort to *vary* them. It worked beautifully for him.

Talk, chat, converse, and communicate. Conversation is the root of all oral communication. The goal of communication is to implant in my mind what's in your mind. And that is done best when you *talk* to me. The burden of the effort is on the communicator. Don't ever forget that. Moving your mouth and saying words in a common language won't be enough.

Work at getting your ideas across. Again, this is the difference between the "Good morning" of small talk and the "Good morning" that sounds like you really mean it. It takes an extra effort. Make that effort.

Be yourself. The *real* you is far more desirable for an audience than the one you think you're supposed to be. Watch carefully the young man who's making a presentation to an audience of successful business people. He's probably going to do exactly the wrong things—try to impress them with his maturity and professionalism rather than to express his ideas clearly, concisely, and simply. You, speaking naturally and with good preparation, are the most impressive person you can be.

Open your face. The open face is the strongest signal an audience can receive that there's warmth, affection, and love motivating the communicator. No body language, no nonverbal communication technique does what the open face does. It's the skill that pays the quickest dividends in audience acceptance.

Smile when appropriate and genuine. Just as you can't pout or throw a tantrum with your brows elevated, you can't look angry, hateful, or oppressive when there's a real, honest-to-goodness smile on your face. It's another wonderful signal of genuine affection, and we can't ever get too much of that.

Gesture when it's comfortable and appropriate. Nothing reaches across the distance between you and your audience like a gesture. Nothing serves as well as a hug without touching. The gesture is the speaker's picture-painting device. It illustrates and emphasizes what you're saying. It demonstrates. So your gestures should be reserved for the highly descriptive words and the strong action words. The open face and the gesture are the two techniques that make the most profound difference in a speaker's acceptance and enjoyment by an audience.

Be open, giving, warm, friendly, and loving. All the other suggestions are wrapped up into this one. When you love your audience, the audience loves you back. That's when communication is at its purest and most perfect. The audience concentrates exclusively on the message it's getting. Again, remember the baby. It doesn't understand your words, but your love sends the signals that are perfect and the message is complete.

Speak in a quiet, conversational voice. This really takes work and concentration until it becomes a habit. A loud voice is a turn-off. It's only successful with young people and their music. Otherwise, loud is offensive. Soft is soothing, comforting, satisfying.

Pause. Trust your audience. They'll wait for you if your pause is effective. It will even heighten their understanding of your message. Don't move your mouth until your mind is in high gear. The pause gives you a chance to think clearly so that what you say will be the best message you can deliver at that moment.

Think silently. Nothing is more frustrating . . . uh . . . than the . . . uh . . . person who . . . uh . . . never gets to the . . . uh . . . end.

Stay calm and reasonable. Nothing is more embarrassing than being in the presence of two people who are screaming at each other. Neither wins your support or your sympathy. The one who appears to be reasonable, sensible, trying to be reassuring usually wins. Let it be you.

Be positive. Just about everyone prefers a "can do" person to a "no can do" one. Also, you can stay out of a lot of trouble by giving information rather than issuing denials, being negative and defensive.

Talk with pride. What a difference pride makes in your attitude and your delivery! Think of the attitude that follows the statements, "I'm proud to be able to tell you" or "Our record speaks for itself. It's the best in our field" as opposed to "We never do that" or "You don't have your facts straight."

Be ready for the worst possible scenario. Be prepared for confrontation. And when someone fires at you, don't immediately fire back. You'll miss unless you pause, look directly at your adversary, think carefully about your reply, and then give a positive answer rather than a defensive reply or a denial. With the possible exception of "When did you stop beating your wife?" almost any question or accusation can be turned in your favor.

Be honest. Yes, there are some people who can lie effectively, but you and I aren't among them. Yes, the truth can be a cause for trouble, but if you tell the truth, you never have to remember what you said. You can never get in as much trouble as the trouble that can be caused by lying. If you can't tell the truth, keep your mouth shut even if people suspect you may be hiding something. The fact is that people love to be told the truth, even if the teller knows he's doing some damage to himself.

Admit "I don't know." It's a key provision of honesty. No one expects you to know everything, but each of us feels "I should know the answer to that," and so we blurt out an answer. Any answer is likely to be either wrong or a lie when you really don't know.

Admit "I don't understand your question." This is another

key to honesty that's harder to accomplish than it sounds. People think they'll appear dumb if they admit to not understanding a question. You'll look even dumber if you give a wrong or inept answer.

Remember your audience at all times. A speaker is not a speaker without an audience. And if an audience likes what it sees and hears, understands you, agrees with you, trusts and believes you, you can be a winner.

Keep eye contact. You're here for your audience. Talk to them. Involve them. When you look at objects instead of people, people grow uninterested if not downright bored. When you look up, you look as if you're asking God for a cue card. When you look down, it appears that you're looking for help from your shoes. Side-to-side movement looks shifty-eyed. Random eye movement suggests fear and uncertainty. Strong eye contact suggests confidence and control.

Concentrate on what you know. You have good information. What you need is time to think about just what that information is and how you can get it across with the greatest impact.

You're the expert. That's the reason you're speaking. You have no cause to feel self-conscious unless you're asked to speak on a subject about which you have very little, insufficient, or no information. In which case, decline, admitting that this is not your area of expertise.

Have confidence in your preparation, your style, and your speaking skill. Fear is your worst enemy. Practicing and using all the speaking skills we have talked about will help you convert crippling fear into energy-producing confidence.

Organize your material. Give your audience the benefit of forethought—prepare. They deserve it. Decide what method of preparation works best for you—outline, notes, manuscript. Take the time to do it right.

Practice aloud. Use recorders, friends, colleagues, a mirror. Use videotape if it's available. It will help you monitor yourself to make sure you're using the techniques you've learned here and to give a dynamite presentation.

Use your text properly. Prepare the words on the paper, using large type and wide margins. Get rid of paper clips and staples. Put your pages in the right order before you get to your feet.

Use simple language. Don't obfuscate. Don't prevaricate. Don't even prioritize in front of a group.

Use short sentences. Ideas with few words are memorable. They're clear and understandable. Nobody likes a windbag.

Be concise. If you can say it in five words, obviously you shouldn't use fifty. Some sentences that can't be improved on are "I love you," "They won," "It's a boy," "You're hired," "Good job," "I'll take it." And as an added bonus, remember this when you're writing letters, proposals, and memos. It works.

Be clear. Figure out how to say what you mean and mean what you say, then do it. Make your sentences the most simple, direct, easy-to-understand statements you can. Far too often people say to other people, "That's not what you said." Often it was what was said, but it wasn't said the best possible way for understanding.

Edit yourself. When you think you're finished preparing, cut, then cut some more. Leave your audience wishing you'd said more rather than wondering why you didn't get off half an hour earlier. Don't be the big snooze. Don't try to tell them everything you know. They don't want to hear it.

Express yourself. Deliver the material in the most dynamic way you can. Stop trying to impress an audience with your body of knowledge. Impress them with how beautifully you deliver your ideas.

Practice the rhythm of eye contact. Your mouth should never be moving while your eyes are looking at the page, the floor, the back wall. As the words flow out, your eyes should be on your audience. Even speakers who know and understand this important principle find that bad habits, fear of losing their place, and fear of the pause cause them to look down toward the paper as they approach the last words of a sentence and to say the first word or two of the next sentence while their eyes are still down. It takes a lot of practice to master this technique because we've been doing it wrong for all the years we've been speaking.

Communicate ideas. One of the hardest traps to overcome is to stop reading words when there's a text in front of you. From now on, stop trying to get exact words from the page. Deliver ideas. Your audience wants to hear what's on your mind, not what's on a piece of paper.

Be attentive to your audience's signals. Just as everything you say and do sends signals to your audience, they're sending you signals all the time. If you see that you're losing them, don't panic. That only makes the situation worse for everyone. Stay calm. If you're well along, it's probably best to wrap it up. If you're at the early part, pull back, concentrate harder on the open face and the gesture, and put more effort into the concept of making intellectual love to your audience. Don't speed up, that's deadly. It tells your audience you want to get it over with. Be more deliberate and offer them more of you. Remember, no one has the right to be dull. When it's all over and you've had a chance to recover, try to analyze *why* you lost their attention so it doesn't happen the next time you have to speak.

Practice diaphragmatic breathing. It's both a speaking tool and a longevity tool. It helps you convert stress into energy. The diaphragm moves out slightly on the inhalation and back in on the exhalation. Remember it. Practice it. It may help keep a heart attack or a stroke from claiming you too soon. It will certainly help you become a more relaxed and natural speaker.

Look and sound pleasant and interesting. The audience has arrived predisposed to like you. Don't turn that around by giving them a reason to tune you out.

Send positive, loving signals. When in doubt, remember again what you do when you speak to a baby. The signals are always right. Use them on an adult audience. Until you're willing to make a fool of yourself in front of an audience, you will.

Be likable. The winner is the person we like. The official who gets elected is the one we like. The likable speaker is the one we believe.

And for every Do in that list, there's a corresponding Don't.

Don't use any of my advice if it doesn't seem natural for you.
Don't make a speech, preach, teach, orate, or pontificate.
Don't imitate anyone else.
Don't frown or look dead.
Don't hide or tie up your hands.
Don't shout or try to reach the back wall.
Don't run on at the mouth.
Don't use sounds to think by. Get rid of all audible pauses.
Don't get angry or uptight.
Don't repeat or reinforce negatives.
Don't be defensive.
Don't wing it.
Don't lie or make it up as you go along.
Don't try to give an answer if you don't understand the question or if you don't know the answer.
Don't repeat a nasty question or ask the questioner to repeat the question.
Don't think about your adversary or yourself.
Don't think "down" or "up" or "away."
Don't assume your audience knows your message.
Don't worry about being too simple.
Don't consider your material dull.
Don't wait until the last minute to prepare.
Don't try to intellectualize everything.
Don't spin your wheels or waste time.

Don't complicate your text.

Don't tell your audience everything you know.

Don't hide behind obscure, technical language.

Don't show off your brilliance.

Don't try to impress the audience.

Don't deliver your talk to your script, the lectern, or your slides.

Don't read words to your audience.

Don't distract or be blatant in speech or dress.

Don't ignore the audience's needs, expectations, or wants.

What your audience needs, expects, and wants is *you*. So *be yourself*.

ACKNOWLEDGMENTS

I owe special thanks to a special group of people:

Hugh McCahey, Forrest P. Lockwood, David Stauffer, and Mills C. Edwards, all former colleagues at the U.S. Chamber of Commerce, and to my assistant, Susan Paynter, for helping me become a writer.

John B. Mannion, Dennis Wholey, Steve Weinberg, and Steve Niven for helping me shape specific chapters.

Patrick O'Connor for the confidence that I could write an appealing hardcover book and for bringing me to the exceptional Simon and Schuster team of Fred Hills, Burton Beals, and Elaine Pfefferblit.

My wife, the novelist Jean Anne Bartlett, and my son, Larry, for giving me organizational and editorial help, for keeping the book moving, for stressing simplicity, and for all the guidance I needed to make me sound in print the way I do in person.

INDEX

and clothing, 69–71
and hands, 62–63
and jewelry, 71–72
at job interview, 128
and reacting, 67–69
and sitting, 65–67, *66*
and standing, 63–65
Sitting, and signals, 65–67, *66*
"60 Minutes" (TV show), 99
Skills, 91–92, 167
and face, 9–17
and gestures, 19–28
at meetings, 135
and mind, 37–51
and voice, 29–35
Smile, 10–11, 165
Speaker, effective, 84, 170
Speech, elements in, 85–86
Stalin, Josef, 47
Standing, and signals, 63–65
"Stiff-upper-lip" smile, 11
St. Louis Post-Dispatch, 43
Stress, 20, 26, 54
and breathing, 58–59
and negotiating, 151
Style, 3–8, 38, 167
and being yourself, 8
and experience, 4–6
at meetings, 135
Sutherland, Joan, 54
Swaggart, Jimmy, 7

Taylor, Elizabeth, 72
Teacher, 40, 143–47
as administrator, 144
as communicator, 144–47
Teacher-student relationship, signals
in, 68
Telephone communication, 33–35
Ten Commandments, 49
Testimony, 111–17
congressional, 114–16
at courtroom trial, 7, 113–14
at deposition, 112–13
at local hearing, 116–17

Text, using properly, 168
"Three Is, The," 158–59
Time
in selling, 160
in television, 100–101
Truman, Harry, State of the Union
Address, 46–48
Truth, value of, 166
TV commercials, 7–8, 26
TV interview, confrontation in, 99–
104
TV news, 43
Twain, Mark, 69
Twenty-third Psalm, 49

United Airlines' pilots strike, 72–73
United Press International, 99

Vishinsky, Andrei, 47
Visual aids, at meetings, 139
Vocal style, 33
Vocal tools, 30–32
pitch, 30–32
rate, 30–32
volume, 30–32
Voice, 29–35, 165
and face, 9–10, 30, 34–35
telephone, 33–35
vocal style, 33
vocal tools, 30–32
Volume, as vocal tool, 30–32

Wallace, Chris, 13
Washington Post, 43
Washington Word Game, 51
Weinberger, Caspar, 94–95
Will, George, 13, 15
Willson, Meredith, 158
Winning signals, *see* Signals
Witness, at courtroom trial, 114
Witness for the Prosecution (film), 111
Words to avoid, 49–50, 85
Writing before speaking, 41–43

Zakharov, Gennadi, 105

ABOUT THE AUTHOR

Arch Lustberg has devoted his professional life to teaching the techniques of effective communication. A former faculty member of the Catholic University of America's renowned Speech and Drama Department, he has been a consultant for six years for the Chamber of Commerce, where he directed the Chamber's Communicator® Workshops, and wrote two best-selling books that were sold exclusively through the Chamber: *Testifying with Impact* and *Winning at Confrontation*. As the head of Arch Lustberg Communications, he coaches business executives, public officials, and professionals in all walks of life on dynamic communication techniques, gives communications workshops and training sessions nationwide, and conducts one of the most popular convention and meeting programs on the circuit. He is based in Washington, D.C.